CHANNEL INFINITE INTELLIGENCE AND
BECOME A VESSEL FOR COSMIC WISDOM

I0453604

CREATIVE
MANIFESTING

◆

II LAWS
OF MANIFESTATION TO AMPLIFY YOUR
INTUITION AND INNER GENIUS

(Law of Attraction, Book 8)

RYUU SHINOHARA

Omen
Publishing

CREATIVE MANIFESTING

How to Get The Most Out of This Book

I see it all the time. Readers devour book after book on the Law of Attraction without ever implementing the transformative insights they've learned. But that's not you. You're here because you want real, lasting change. This book is your tool for manifesting that change. To ensure you truly embody the principles in these pages, I've created exclusive resources that will supercharge your journey.

These bonuses are designed to help you take immediate action and create the results you desire. Don't let this knowledge go to waste—unlock your bonuses now and begin manifesting the life of your dreams.

>> Scan the QR Code below to get your free bonuses <<

Free Bonus #1: MNTALITY Collective –
Where Mindset Meets Mastery

Join a powerful community of like-minded individuals who are transforming their lives. The **MNTALITY Collective** offers a space for growth, collaboration, and inspiration. As a member, you'll gain access to weekly livestreams covering topics including personal development, scaling your business, and manifesting new opportunities. Whichever path you choose, this community is here to support you every step of the way.

Free Bonus #2: Manifester Master List

Discover the top 3 daily habits that master manifesters swear by. This checklist includes actionable steps you can implement immediately to speed up your manifestations, and a simple tracking layout to monitor your progress. Start turning your vision into reality today.

Free Bonus #3: Intention Journal

Feel like journaling takes too long? This Intention Journal is designed for efficiency. In under a minute, you'll align your mind and energy to your highest intentions using just a few powerful prompts. Get the clarity and focus you need to start every day with purpose.

Free Bonus #4: Four Subtle Meditation Mistakes to Avoid

If you are among the millions of people who meditate, you know that roadblocks can arise that frustrate your ability to remain in an uninterrupted meditative state. This guide uncovers the four most common mistakes that keep you from entering a deep meditative state. Learn how to bypass these pitfalls and truly harness the full power of your meditation practice.

Free Bonus #5: Meditation Design Blueprint

Explore the most effective, time-tested structure for deepening your meditative state. With this step-by-step meditation guide, you amplify your alignment with the universe and become the most empowered version of yourself.

Free Bonus #6: Four Anti-Manifestation Practices

Without realizing it, many people engage in practices that actually work *against* them. This guide will help you identify these sneaky, counterproductive habits and show you how to shift them into the frequency of your goals so you can manifest with ease.

Free Bonus #7: Four-Step Conscious Business Acceleration

If you're an entrepreneur or business owner, you know the unique challenges that come with building a conscious, aligned business. This four-step blueprint helps you experience quantum leaps in your financial success, all while staying true to your highest vision.

Extra Bonus: Unlock the Quantum Meditation Audio

For those who join the **MNTALITY Collective**, there's an extra surprise waiting for you! This **Quantum Meditation Audio** guides you into a profound state of awareness, helping you tap into the quantum field and align with your highest potential. This powerful tool is reserved exclusively for community members.

Table of Contents

Introduction

I never saw myself as a creative person. Growing up, I was encouraged to explore art, starting with preschool paintings of my family—egg-shaped heads, sausage arms, and block legs. When I turned eleven, my dad bought a drum set for Nico and me. Every Saturday, I walked to the neighbor's house for drumming lessons and eventually learned *Last Resort* by California rock band, Papa Roach. But despite consistent practice, my drumming didn't lead anywhere. After a year, I quit, and my dad sold the set.

A few years later, I took guitar as an elective in high school. Like most freshmen, I was picking the easiest classes and "most chill" professors. I learned a few chords here and there, but nothing really stuck. Everything I'd learned about the guitar eventually faded into distant memory, unrecoverable.

My lukewarm attempts at creating extended to writing. I didn't write for enjoyment until I was twenty-two. Before then, I wrote to satisfy teachers and meet school requirements. Writing as a career felt like a far-off idea; I associated it with books I didn't want to read, political debates I didn't care to debate, or hypothetical problems I didn't need to solve.

Though I tried creating in different ways, it never felt natural. I thought I lacked talent, that I was just mediocre or not good enough at anything I attempted. After a string of failed attempts, negative thoughts started to creep in.

"Maybe I wasn't meant to stand out."

"Maybe I was born to be average."

My thinking shifted when I dove into spirituality and personal development. Suddenly, everything and nothing made sense—I learned about the universal laws and realized how little I truly understood. From there, I dedicated myself to learning and applied every technique I came across: mindset exercises, belief-building methods, and mental reprogramming practices. These helped me quiet a substantial portion of my insecurities, limiting beliefs, and negative self-talk. I'd once been a broke, insecure, lonely university student, but with guidance from inspired writers, motivational speakers, and new thought teachers, I broke out of my shell. My failed attempts at drawing, making music, writing, and expressing myself through sports or academics weren't due to a lack of talent—they stemmed from mental blocks and not understanding my true nature.

It wasn't that I lacked talent—I just wasn't skilled in what I pursued. It wasn't that I lacked creativity—I just wasn't passionate about what I was making. It wasn't that I could never be extraordinary—I just hadn't granted myself permission to step into that role.

Creativity is not something you have or don't have. It's something every single person can channel and discover through self-mastery.

Discover Your Gift

The right person, with the right mindset, creates magic. Your favorite song, movie, book, painting, or product was crafted by someone who poured their heart into their work. Regular people—just like you and me—created them all. But have you ever noticed that two people can perform the same song with the same lyrics and instruments, yet have completely different results? One becomes a superstar, while the other fades into the background. What sets them apart? The answer: Nothing.

Many of us spend our lives doing things we weren't meant to do. Imagine a singer working an office job because of low self-esteem. Or a pastry chef who joined the police academy because they didn't have the funds for culinary school. Or a writer pursuing a degree in engineering only because math was their best subject growing up (me). Every day, external influences steer people away from their power because they lack the clarity, confidence, or resources to pursue their heart's calling.

To be a creator, we must cultivate creativity. It's no surprise that those who transcend ordinary thinking often build lucrative businesses, craft impactful art, and develop products that reshape the world. By discovering your unique gift and unlocking the full potential of the most powerful tool we all possess—the mind—you can align with your most creative self. In doing so, you'll bring to life the dream you've always envisioned.

Through my studies, I realized that talent, skill, and creativity are accessible to everyone—including you. You possess a unique gift capable of transforming lives, whether hundreds, thousands, or even millions. In this book, we'll dive into how to tap into your greatest abilities and make the impact you're destined for.

Stop Looking for Your Purpose

Lance Armstrong, a young, talented athlete, had everything going for him in the early 90s as he pursued greatness in the cycling world. Suddenly, in October 1996, he was diagnosed with testicular cancer, which spread to his lungs, abdomen, and brain. For the next year and a half, Lance underwent an extensive series of surgeries and chemotherapy. In 1997, he was declared cancer-free and returned to his lifelong passion.

Following his recovery, he won the Tour de France seven times from 1999 to 2005. Lance became an icon for cancer patients worldwide. But his drive to inspire and promote strength, belief, and perseverance blinded him, and in 2012, he was found guilty of using PED (Performance-Enhancing Drugs) dating back to the mid-90s. These drugs were essential in helping him attain his success. The U.S. Anti-Doping Agency stripped him of all seven titles and banned him from professional cycling.

Lance Armstrong is the perfect example of someone who put unnecessary weight on their shoulders to pursue a "greater purpose." It backfired. While his cause was noble, his reasons were ego driven. Anything manifested from the ego has a shaky foundation and is bound to fail.

Stop looking for your purpose. Every time you look for something (especially something as important as your purpose), you'll sprinkle it with bits and pieces of bias, conditioning, and ego. Nobody wants their purpose to be anything that isn't what they expect it to be. Everybody would love to be someone's hero. The reality is you only need to be a hero for yourself—that's how you help others be their own hero, too.

Instead of looking for your purpose, listen to it. After all, it's called your *calling*. Your highest excitements, greatest passions, and creative visions should fuel your decision-making, not some artificially generated idea that looks nice on paper.

When we operate from a state of lack or desperation, we tend to rush or force outcomes. Forcing an outcome makes us ignore the process—and when the process of creating a work of art, product, service, community, or anything else is ignored, it's rooted in greed and taking. Trying to manipulate your way to success never lasts, and leads to something that lacks real value. The best "marketing" you can do for anything you create is to make it the best it can be. This means aligning yourself with a greater cosmic wisdom, going beyond ordinary thoughts, and tapping into extraordinary levels of creativity. When you find the right path, the right outcomes follow naturally. This book isn't about manifesting epic outcomes but about discovering the path that leads to them.

Want to live a life that's freeing? Follow your highest excitement. Don't do what you think you need to do. Do what you're inspired to do. This is how you find your purpose, channel infinity, and tap into your inner genius. It's difficult to find your purpose when you're forcing yourself to learn a skill or faking passion for something you don't care about. The simplest way to find your purpose is by allowing the Universe to create through you instead of trying to impose your will onto it. When you become a vessel for the Universe to create, you manifest from a place of limitless creativity and divine Intelligence—this is what it means to be authentic. Become the greatest version of who you are, and not a watered-down replica of someone you saw on TV.

Be Who You Are

Most people don't realize that when they're truly authentic, life unfolds with greater ease. Manifesting can feel long and exhausting because we spend so much energy wearing masks. We fake interests, hold back words, suppress emotions, and try to match others' expectations. It's a draining way to live.

The alternative? Let go of what you think you *should* do, and follow what you feel called to do. Get crystal clear on what makes you feel alive—it's the key to unlocking everything you want. Find a passion so powerful that you'd pursue it for life, even if it shatters others' expectations.

I can hear you wondering, "But what about money? I need to make a living."

This mindset is often called the "broke artist" trap—the belief that following your passion means sacrificing abundance. But that's simply not true. When you truly have talent and passion for something, you'll find a way to make it work—even if it requires sacrifices early on. When I first started writing, I lived with my parents, had no social life, and let go of most hobbies. My obsession was learning metaphysics, teaching others, and sharing my message.

I'd occasionally meet up with old friends, who'd joke that I was "living in a cave." In a way, I was. But it wasn't for nothing. It was to create a lifestyle aligned with my values and talents. Today, I wake up without an alarm, travel freely, and create content around topics I could explore forever. Now, they ask, "How did you do it?"

Even if you can't immediately make a living from your creations, they're still worth exploring. You can have both a day job and a passion project—one doesn't have to exclude the other. Being creative is more than reaching an outcome; it's about aligning your mind and heart with your soul and expressing that to the world in whatever form it takes. Your purpose doesn't need to be your income source; it needs to be the thing that brings you fulfillment. And by doing things that bring you fulfillment, you naturally align with the frequency of your best life.

When you feel called to something, don't let outside influences make you feel crazy or delusional. This book will help you identify your "one thing" and profit from it, so you can live your passion while meeting life's demands.

Creative Manifesting is more than a manifestation guide. It's about finding a path so fulfilling that you don't focus on making the immaterial material. In doing so, you'll attract everything you could ever want. By stepping outside the game of egos, you'll make space for the divine to flood your life with abundance I can hardly describe—but I'll try. The journey to amplifying your intuition and inner genius begins here.

CHAPTER 1

Source of Infinity

◆◆◆

LAW #1:

Everything Is One

As long as the tree is behind you, you can see only its shadow.
If you want to touch reality, you have to turn around.
— **Master Tai Xu**

One morning in Alaska, a farmer was going on a morning hike in the mountains when he came across an eagle's egg. Not knowing what it was, he took it to his farm and placed it in the chicken coop. When the baby eagle hatched, surrounded by chickens and unaware of its nature, it adopted the traits, habits, and behaviors of a chicken. It pecked at the ground like a chicken. It tried to cluck to communicate like a chicken. It stayed on the ground, never spreading its wings to fly—just like a chicken.

We are all eagles behaving like chickens. We accept the bare minimum and pursue a fraction of what we're capable of—not because we lack resources, information, or connections, but because we don't know our true nature. If you knew your entire life you were an eagle, you wouldn't be living like a chicken.

The Origin of Creation

For millennia, humanity has pondered the nature of reality. As we evolved from small hunter-gatherer tribes to vast civilizations, we gained the freedom and security to explore life's grandest questions: Where did all of this come from? Who, or what, created this? Who created us? When we ask these questions, the answers often seem elusive, as if hidden just beyond reach.

"It was the gods," some might say. But even answers like these only lead to more questions. "Okay, but who are the gods? And who created them?"

Our curiosity about our nature and purpose runs deep because we are purpose-driven beings, motivated by an instinctual desire for evolution and expansion. It's in our DNA to plant seeds, leave a legacy, and strive for something beyond mere survival. Biologically, we may just be highly conscious primates, yet spiritually, we sense there's so much more. We long to explain why we stand apart from every other creature in the animal kingdom.

In recent centuries, science has offered theories—Evolution, the Big Bang—that suggest we're nothing more than freak accidents, products of a fortuitous convergence of elements. I don't buy it.

Could everything we've created so far—our civilizations, innovations, and understanding—truly stem from such a rudimentary reason for existence? Could humanity have survived and thrived for so long without some connection to a higher consciousness? Perhaps there's more to our existence, something science hasn't yet been able to capture.

To answer these questions, humanity turned to religion, which historically began with animism and totemism—a way to understand and connect with the spiritual realm. Ancient tribes saw every element of the natural world as alive and possessing a soul. Certain animals, plants, and places, like a mountain or a lake, were revered as spiritually significant. This belief evolved over time, with each culture identifying specific gods who governed aspects of human life, creating a framework through which we could reconcile with forces greater than ourselves.

Fast forward to the ancient civilizations of the Sumerians, Babylonians, Assyrians, Egyptians, Greeks, and Romans, where a multitude of gods were believed to rule every aspect of life and nature. These pagan deities formed the spiritual backbone of their societies, each god governing elements like war, love, harvest, or the sea.

Then came Emperor Constantine, who saw the unifying potential of Christianity and, in a strategic move, declared it the official religion of the Roman Empire. This not only strengthened his grip over the empire but reshaped the spiritual landscape of the Western world. And the rest, as they say, is history.

Through sharing stories, analogies, and anecdotes, humans developed faith in things supernatural. For example, Genesis describes how God spoke the word and created the heavens and the earth in six days. Buddhism often refers to how the Universe is cyclical, with not one beginning but multiple—moving through the process of birth, death, and rebirth (Samsara). In Taoism, the Universe is born from the Tao, an undefinable force and the source of everything—leading to the rise of yin and yang, whose interactions led to creation. In Greek mythology, the Universe began with Chaos, leading to the creation of Gaia (the Earth), Tartarus (the Underworld), and Eros (Love).

Every religion and philosophy has its own story. Despite their differences, they all have one belief in common: the source of the Universe is conscious. For believers, the creation of the heavens and earth was not a conglomerate of random events. The Universe began with a Cause that gave birth to Spirit—the source through which everything is created. Spirit is conscious, self-knowing, and all-knowing. If this were not the case, there would be no impulse to move and create. Spirit is all, and there is nothing else but itself. Therefore, it moves upon itself and creates everything from itself.

Things that are seen were not made of things which do appear.
—Hebrews 11:3

Spirit operates with Intelligence and its purpose is to create. Some seekers refer to this as God—the conscious creator of All That Is. This Intelligence creates everything with the power of the Word. This generates an activity of Intelligence, making the non-manifest turn into manifest, the invisible turn into the visible.

If all is Spirit, then we are Spirit and one with this Intelligence. We create with the Word (thought) the world we see with our eyes. We are the conscious creators of this ever-expanding Universe. You could say, "We are gods in the flesh."

The Purpose of Spirit

Spirit has one purpose: To know itself. To do this, It must have freedom, for without freedom, there would be limits, and with limits, It can't know itself. Remember, Spirit IS all that is. Freedom is the bedrock of the creative act.

Humans are born with a brain, the biological organ that facilitates our experience of the mind. While the brain processes information via neurons, tissues, and chemicals, the mind is the gateway to consciousness, giving us the ability to generate or channel new ideas. It has the remarkable power and freedom to think any thought, imagine any image, and visualize any scene. Through this dynamic interaction, we access a unique inner world, unconstrained by physical reality, enabling us to create, wonder, and explore possibilities beyond the tangible.

Before anything manifests, it already exists as a potential. The same goes for any idea. When an idea comes to mind, it already exists pre-thought. In other words, before ideas manifest in the mind, they already exist within a field of infinite information and potential. This field contains all possible realities, even before they are thought. We are creators in the sense that we bring to being that which is dormant in unmanifested potential.

The mind is one tool through which Spirit gets to know itself. We can connect to an infinite number of probable realities. Anything that is yet to exist physically already exists mentally. And anything that is yet to exist mentally already exists meta-physically. Human beings have the unique gift of being able to tap into an endless reservoir of creative potential.

This is the potential that began composing *Requiem*, painted the Mona Lisa, launched Google, and is writing this book right now. Everything you see around you was created from it. This potential is something you've already been tapping into. You've been using this power your entire life. It's not something you need to "learn" or "start doing." You're already there. You are everything you need to be to attract, create, and manifest everything you want.

Everything is one. You are one with this creative potential and divine Intelligence. Recognize your true nature. Be responsible for your thinking. Whether one is aware of the creative potential of one's own Spirit, and whether one takes charge of the creative process, we are all still creating and we are all still planting the seeds for creation. Thoughts are things—and we reap what we sow. Whether we are happy or we are suffering, Spirit knows itself through us.

Spirit is neutral in the way it expands. This is why we can think of freedom as a curse. It gives us responsibility over our thoughts. For many people, this is too much to handle. We outsource this responsibility to the external world (or something outside of ourselves), and we fall into patterns of victimhood, drama, and self-pity.

We human beings don't lack creative potential. We fear it. Especially when it comes to our passion and calling. We're so afraid of the potential of who we could be, we'd rather sit in the familiarity of the persona into which others have molded us. To change this, get into the habit of recognizing your true nature.

You are me. I am you. You are everything around you. Nothing is separate. It all stems from the same source: Spirit. Recognizing this source is the gateway to expansive and creative thinking. As you peek through the clouds, the sky reveals itself. The more you see, the more it opens up. Before you know it, you'll see the light.

Recognition

Awakening begins with recognizing your own power. The more you acknowledge this power, the more you're willing to take responsibility for it. Recognition is the key to awakening, and to stay awake, you must cultivate the habit of continuous recognition. Each moment of awareness strengthens your connection to your true potential.

If you're unaware of your true nature, why would you take risks, try something new, or do something extraordinary? A limited definition of self creates a limited reality. A plant will never grow bigger than the pot that it's in. Similarly, a mind will never receive thoughts and ideas beyond the contents of the limiting beliefs it holds. To expand your thinking, you must expand your perception of your potential.

Many people don't improve their thinking because they're unaware of how it shapes their reality. They don't realize the power of a single thought. It's like playing an Atari game on a MacBook Pro—you have the processing power for 4K resolution with stunning graphics, yet you settle for 2D pixels. Reality has nuances and layers that require a sharper, more expansive perception. Without this, you miss out on the profound truths embedded in your experiences.

If you don't know where you come from, you won't understand the language of success. You could read all the books and listen to all the advice from those who have successfully manifested their dreams, but you'd never notice the genuine message between the lines. There's a magnetic energy underlying every successful individual. This is the energy most people cloud, hold back, or cover up out of fear of what it can reveal if they were to open up their heart to the world.

If you were to unleash this authentic energy, you'd be labeled as "delusional," "out of touch with reality," or, my favorite, "selfish." Following your heart's greatest calling has no place in environments created to nurture limited thinkers. Don't get me wrong. There's a time and place for rationality that can accompany a limiting mindset, but not when it comes at the cost of creativity and happiness.

Not everyone becomes a successful artist, painter, writer, musician, actor, businessperson, or entrepreneur. If you look around you, this is clear. For ninety-nine percent of people, it's not because they lack the resources, talent, or support. It's because many of them don't even try! And if they try and fail, they don't try again. As I've often said, manifestation is a lifestyle, not an end goal. It's the process of consistently seeking and living true to your highest values and excitement. In doing so, you manifest a life in alignment with your greatest purpose, passions, and gifts.

Summary for Chapter 1: The Source of Infinity
Law #1: Everything Is One

- **The Eagle and Chicken Analogy**: We often live below our potential, like an eagle raised as a chicken, unaware of its true power. This reflects how limiting beliefs keep us small.

- **Creation from Consciousness**: Various spiritual traditions, despite their differences, agree that the Universe was created from a conscious source (Spirit, God, the Tao). The activity of Intelligence led to creation of everything we see.

- **Spirit's Purpose Is Self-Knowledge**: Spirit's purpose is to know itself, which requires freedom. Without freedom, there would be no creative expansion.

- **We Are Co-Creators**: As conscious beings, we are one with Spirit and are always manifesting—whether intentionally or unintentionally. Our thoughts are the seeds of creation.

- **Freedom Brings Responsibility:** Every thought holds creative potential, and with freedom comes the power—and responsibility—to choose which thoughts we nurture with our attention and energy.

- **The Practice of Recognition**: Consistently recognizing your true nature as a co-creator is the key to tapping into your creative potential and intuition.

- **Manifestation as a Lifelong Process**: Manifestation is not a single event but a continuous process of aligning with Spirit, amplifying your intuition, and manifesting through inspired action.

Journaling Prompts

- **Recognizing Your True Nature:** Reflect on a moment in your life when you felt a deep connection to something greater than yourself. How did this experience challenge your previously held beliefs and perspectives?

- **Fear of Responsibility:** In what area in your life are you avoiding responsibility, assigning fault, or pointing the finger? Knowing this can provide clarity about where you feel disempowered.

- **Aligning with Universal Desire:** How can you align your daily actions with this desire for growth and self-knowledge? The active pursuit of learning brings you closer to your true self.

Exercises

- **Daily Cosmic Connection:** Every morning for the next week, spend five minutes in silence, recognizing that you are one with everything and connected to an infinite supply of creative potential. Set an intention to recognize and channel creative potential throughout the day.

CHAPTER 2

Channel Infinity

LAW #2:

We Are Vessels for the Universe

We are the music makers, and we are the dreamers of dreams.
— **Arthur O'Shaughnessy**

I grew up a gamer. For many years, gaming was my idea of "having fun." Sitting in front of a computer monitor or TV screen, alone or with friends, was how I enjoyed a big chunk of my leisure time. I played every type of game—sports, survival, arcade, etc. Each game came with unique challenges, speeds, and play styles (oh, and let's not forget, frustrations, too). Despite the variety, my favorite part of any video game was always the customization aspect.

Customization enhances the gaming experience. It allows the player to create a character representing their personality and style, increasing their personal investment and making the game more engaging and enjoyable. Life is like a video game. We customize ourselves with the clothes we wear, the people we hang around with, the places we go, the career path we take, and even the haircut we choose (or don't choose) to get. You can create any character you want, which directly influences your reality. There are infinite ways to customize your reality to your personal taste. Yet, most people don't engage in this way. We limit our self-expression, hide our true selves, and allow the game to come as it is. Most of us live in default mode. We give the controller to someone else. So, if we're not playing the game, who is?

The Illusion of Limitation

Everyone fights for freedom but doesn't know what to do when they get it. Throughout human history, countless revolutions and wars have occurred in the name of freedom, many of them justified. We don't like the idea of being chained. We're spiritual beings, after all, and deep down, we know we're meant for more. Whenever an obstacle prevents us from fulfilling a desired potential, we do everything possible to remove it. We raise our fists and defend with everything we have the freedom to make our own choices and walk our own paths. But freedom comes with a cost: *responsibility*.

How many people take advantage of our hard-earned freedom? You have the freedom to get into the best shape of your life, so why not do it? You have the freedom to study frantically and become above average in any subject in less than six months, so why not do it? You have the freedom to practice public speaking all day long until you can inspire a crowd like Tony Robbins, so why not do it?

When we recognize our true nature, it's empowering—it's a moment of truth and awakening. We feel inspired and light, as though we've been reborn. We feel an impulse to do something with this newfound energy, but the magic is fleeting. Self-imposed expectations rise, pressure builds, and fear of criticism from friends and family creeps in. Then it happens: The ego latches on to our spiritual pursuit.

The ego attempts to rationalize everything, planting seeds of limitation in every step along our journey. We intellectualize experiences that are inheritably spontaneous and intuitive, limiting ourselves to a small reservoir of creative potential. Rather than using our freedoms to channel infinity, we play it safe and narrow ourselves to predictable, expected paths. *We bind ourselves with our own freedom.*

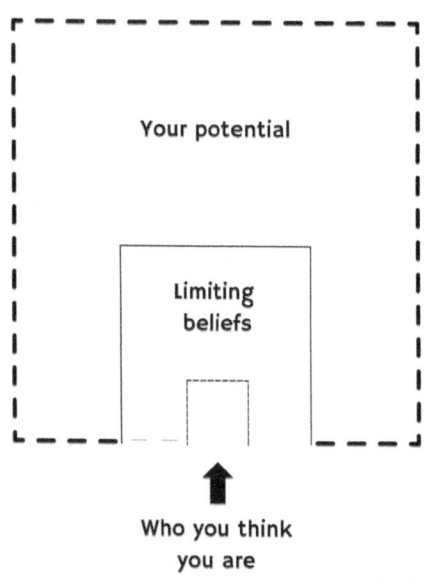

Creating from the mind is like creating from a puzzle. You can create only one image—the story of the ego. It's the known creating the known. Creating from the heart and Spirit is like putting together a never-ending puzzle. You attach one piece to another until you have this fantastic picture aligned with your personal preferences. In order to become a vessel for the Universe, you need to trust that the right pieces of the puzzle will come together. Without trust, you manifest expectations, but you never exceed them.

There's a biological reason we limit ourselves with our freedom. Without a filter through which we experience reality, we'd be overwhelmed with information. This is the part of the brain called the reticular activating system (RAS). It focuses our attention and energy on a few essentials, allowing us to navigate effectively through reality. Instead of spreading our attention thin across multiple memories, ideas, and events all at once, the RAS pinpoints the most important task at the moment.

For example, when you hear your name in a loud room full of people with music playing in the background, your name stands out because it's the most important word in your mind. However, we've overexploited this mechanism over time, narrowing our focus excessively and losing touch with our innate sense of wonder and adventure.

Our minds fear the creative potential our heart desires to express. We've been conditioned to keep things "realistic" and "rational" and not go beyond the reality the mind has labeled as "my life." But here's the thing. If we want to create a new reality with more abundance, joy, and fulfillment, we need to go *beyond*. Otherwise, we'll keep creating the same scenes repeatedly.

There is so much we can do, see, and create, yet we don't do any of it. It's not because we lack freedom—it's because we have too much of it! Limitation is an illusion—it's sometimes helpful to keep us safe and secure, but not when it stifles your creativity.

Heart-Centered Creativity

The process of creation is less about thinking and more about feeling. I understand that whenever I create something from scratch, whether it's a book, video, course, or business, I always try to channel inspiration from my heart. When we think our way into creativity, we can experience writer's block, analysis paralysis, and creative burnout. Although brilliant in its nature, the thinking mind has boundaries, mechanisms, and conditions that prevent it from coming up with expansive, extraordinary ideas. The theme of this chapter is not about creating, but about *channeling*.

Many of history's most successful artists have attributed their creativity and impact to the passion, emotion, and authenticity in their work. Giants like Bob Dylan, J. K. Rowling, and Pablo Picasso all ascribed their creativity to a source of inspiration beyond what the mind can comprehend. Whether you are a musician, writer, or painter, or you work in another medium, when you approach your work from a pure place, everything you create will have a magnetic pull. It'll be sprinkled with irreplaceable energy. For example, readers tell me that when they read my books, they feel my energy.

When I published my first book, I hired a creative writer to help me. This person added stories, analogies, and examples to flesh out my ideas and concepts. After completing my first draft, I sent it over to my editor. A few days later, we got on a call to talk about the book. She said the book was great. The ideas were thoughtful and practical, but something was off. She said, "It feels like two people are writing this book. Is someone else helping you?" From that moment on, I knew I couldn't fake my energy. Others may express themselves similarly, but their words feel different. My art had to be something I created myself, from my soul.

Today, many people outsource their creative power to Artificial Intelligence. AI uses content that *already exists* and repackages it. Just like the mind, it creates knowns from knowns. No matter how powerful AI becomes, it will never replace human creativity. It can replicate, model, and support the creative process, but it can never replace artists. And that's because *AI has no soul.*

Have you ever read an AI-generated text or looked at an AI-generated picture? They're easy to recognize once you've seen a few. Will AI get better with time? I don't doubt it. But no matter how good it gets, its creations will always lack soul. Even if someone were to invent a state-of-the-art, million-dollar 3D food printer, it would never replace mom's home-cooked meals because the printer is missing the secret ingredient: Love.

Last year, I spent a few weeks at my grandma's house in Costa Rica, just minutes from the beach. Every morning, she'd pour my grandpa and me a cup of coffee—the best I've ever tasted. It was a blend of locally grown Costa Rican beans, two spoons of coconut oil, and a hint of stevia, whipped together until a light foam formed on top. After showing me the process, I tried it myself. I measured the coffee, counted the spoons of oil, timed the blending, but it never tasted quite like hers. Was it just practice? Or maybe "talent"? Such a simple recipe, yet no matter how close I got, it never matched the taste and sweetness that came from her hands.

There's a reason love songs and romance books have always been at the top of the music and book charts. People connect with love. They connect with emotion. Love is a Universal theme. When you speak from the soul, you're speaking to every soul. Remember, we're all one. When you create from a place of wanting to help, inspire, and move others, you create from oneness. This is the purest path to creating anything. When you create from a place of ego, your impact is limited—and unsustainable. Without a deeper, underlying interest or passion, everything you produce will feel lackluster and amateur.

True professionals are passionate. They don't bother working on things they're not interested in. They understand that nothing significant will ever come without an inner fire. This inner fire is necessary to spark revolution and innovation. It's the source of global movements and societal shifts—it makes people feel happy, clear, and connected.

When you operate from the heart, you're connecting with the Divine. We are vessels. The goal of the artist is not to create, but to allow creation to happen through them. An artist must be disciplined in their work, master their technique, and prepare their mind and heart to be ready when inspiration strikes. Talent cannot compensate for a closed heart or a limited mind. Inspiration strikes everyone, but only those who are prepared can channel it effectively. For everyone else, it'll be like winning the lottery but not having a bank account to receive the deposit. Live from a receptive, open state while mastering your craft. This is how you channel creative potential into material things.

Throughout this book, we'll cover principles and techniques for tapping into heart-centered creativity so you can make the impact only you can make. When authenticity becomes the foundation through which you manifest things into reality, doors will open for you.

The Frequency of Authenticity

In a world plagued with filters, scams, and AI, those who show signs of humanness and relatability stand out. Over the past twenty years, we've been bombarded with overly edited propaganda to the point of desensitization. The everyday media consumer has become skeptical of perfection. Having a Lamborghini, dating a Russian-model girlfriend, or throwing parties on your own yacht are no longer attractive to most people. We've learned to see through the façade.

For example, Instagram used to be dominated by curated, picture-perfect lifestyle posts. Many Instagram users were monetizing their posts by partnering with companies to post brand-specific products that earned them cash. The problem was, they promoted products that didn't align with theirs or their followers' values. Constant exposure to everyday media consumers and dissatisfaction of customers led to an increase in cynicism. Engagement and performance dropped as people no longer resonated with this style of publicity. Who can blame them? Many of social media's most viral clips in recent times have come from regular, everyday people showing more of who they are and less of what they're not. Authenticity is, and always has been, magnetic and attractive.

In the beauty and fashion industry, consumers have increasingly demanded authenticity. Many personal care brands have responded by moving away from airbrushed models and unattainable beauty portrayals—what was once the industry standard has been turned on its head. Companies realized that consumers no longer trusted these idealized images, prompting a shift to more authentic depictions of beauty. Brands that embraced this change regained credibility and continue to attract a broader audience by celebrating real, relatable beauty.

Another example of the power of authenticity can be seen in local brick-and-mortar businesses. A mom-and-dad shop with a bit of personality, creativity, and a wonderful product will go viral and have people waiting in line the next day. This happened to a bookstore in Los Angeles called Skylight Books. Like many businesses, they faced challenges because of the rise of internet shopping and the impact of the pandemic. Despite this, the store's unique charm, cozy environment, and passionate staff attracted the eye of one TikTok user who posted about them. This clip went viral, and Skylight Books' online and offline orders soared nationwide.

The rising demand for authenticity reflects a global rise in consciousness. The more detached we are from our ego, the less we resonate with ego-centered creators, art, and businesses. Authenticity has become leading edge.

The more you embrace who you are, the more you can attract. The frequency of authenticity is in alignment with the Universe. When you allow yourself to be as you are, you become a vessel for creation. You no longer impose your ego desires onto the Universe—you allow a Universal desire to express itself through you. As I pointed out earlier, the Universe is a source of infinite ideas waiting to be manifested in the physical world. All you have to do is surrender to the creative flow and tap into that boundless resource—that's how you channel infinity.

Channeling creative potential isn't about relying on finite tools like memory, identity, or algorithms—it's about opening your heart. When you pursue what genuinely resonates with you, you unlock a level of fulfillment, joy, and freedom beyond what the mind alone can conceive. The mind may be limited, but the heart taps into the boundless. The right people, opportunities, and ideas will flow into your life the moment you let your heart take the driver's seat.

Become One of One

Remember, we're all one. We're all connected. We're all a creation from the same source. Therefore, something that resonates and connects with your soul will resonate with the soul of others. Most people don't know who they are, but when they see someone expressing their authentic gifts and truth, it reminds them of their own. This is how you create a movement.

By discovering who you are, you can become the most magnetic version of you for everyone to see. In a world polluted with filters, deep-fakes, AI-generated content, and overly edited clips, anything that is authentic will stick out. If you want to stand out, learn to stand in. Your story is your advantage. Nobody can be you. By embracing this concept, you'll realize just how easy it is to create.

For example, when I first started my daily email newsletter, I struggled. I spent a lot of time trying to "come up with ideas" so I could create something I thought people would like. Then a mentor told me, "Stop trying to come up with ideas. They're all around you. *Everything is email content.*" He was right. If all I did was write about my daily experiences, like a journal entry, not only would it be easier to create, but it would be more entertaining. My audience would connect with my story and who I am—and as a result, my content would resonate with the right audience.

The moment you realize YOU are the source of inspiration, everything changes. There is no more competition because nobody can be you, and your life becomes a blue ocean of opportunity. You stop looking outside for ideas and you look at your own life experiences. All the struggles you've been through, the successes you've had, the things you've learned, and the people you've met—even that extraordinary experience you had on a random Tuesday—become your source of inspiration. People don't follow products and services. They follow a story. They follow a mission. They follow other people. To stand out, stand in.

Summary for Chapter 2: Channel Infinity
Law #2: We Are Vessels for the Universe

- **Life is Customizable:** Just like in a video game, you can customize your reality, but many people limit their self-expression and live in "default mode."

- **The Illusion of Limitation:** While freedom offers boundless opportunities, many of us impose self-limitations out of fear or habit.

- **Heart-Centered Creativity:** True creation comes from the heart, not the mind. The mind can only replicate what's known, while the heart channels infinite Intelligence.

- **The Ego's Interference:** The ego latches onto our creative endeavors, limiting our creative potential with rationalizations and expectations.

- **We are Interconnected:** When you speak from the soul, you're speaking to all souls. This interconnectedness makes soul driven ideas more magnetic and impactful.

- **The Power of Authenticity:** In a world full of filters, AI, and over-edited content, authenticity is valued now more than ever. Authenticity is the leading edge.

- **You Are the Source:** Your life experiences, stories, and authenticity are your greatest assets. Embrace them to stand out in a world that craves realness.

Journaling Prompts

- **Exploring Your Authenticity:** Reflect on a moment in your life when you felt most connected to your true self. What was different about that experience? How can you bring more of that authenticity into your creative work?

- **Listening to Your Heart:** What is your heart calling you to create? Write a list of things you've intuitively wanted to create your entire life.

- **Your Differentiator:** Write a list of unique characteristics, quirks, or talents you feel make you different from everyone else. How can you integrate these into your creative process?

Exercises

- **Daily Heart-Centered Practice:** Each morning, take five minutes to quiet your mind and listen to your heart. Without filtering them, write down ideas, thoughts, or feelings that emerge.

- **Authenticity Challenge:** Choose one area of your life where you feel you're not expressing your true self. Over the next week, attempt to show up authentically in that area.

CHAPTER 3

The Sound of Limitation

LAW #3:

Noise Clouds Creativity

We all wear masks, and the time comes when we cannot remove them
without removing some of our own skin.

— **André Berthiaume**

A confused creator can't tell the difference between their voice and the voice of others. This is the biggest block to creativity. When you lose yourself in outside noise, the internal has no peace and is silenced.

Before we jump into this chapter, let's define "noise." We'll use the word noise to describe everything that isn't your truth, and all the false desires society has implanted in you since you were young. Noise is the criticism and hate that happens all over social media. It's your ego's need to compare itself with others, and the judgy looks that come from family and friends when you try something new. It's the opinions of so-called "experts" in your field or industry that make you doubt yourself and your ideas. It's the unrealistic standards of advertisers convincing you that you're not good enough unless you have XYZ. Noise is everything that derails you from what you were born to do.

The World Is Loud

The noise of the outside world is loud and persuasive. Ten seconds of scrolling through social media is equivalent to having ten people come up to you and tell you their opinions, stories, or unsolicited advice. It finds its way into your head. You believe your thoughts because you think they're coming from you when, in reality, they're a cluster of other people's thoughts.

However, since it's happening through a device, we think we have a choice about whether we accept the information. Here's what we often forget: *everything is being captured,* filling up space in your mind. Without you even realizing it, all the information you consume, whether or not beneficial, is implanted in your subconscious mind, clouding your creative potential and inner guidance. The effects can be long-lasting.

Confused creators invest in projects not because they're passionate about them, but because someone said they'll get something out of it. We pursue goals thinking they're ours when really, they're societal expectations and standards. We stand behind certain values not because they define us, but because we think it's the moral thing to do. The noise can shape your identity—and if it can shape your identity, it can shape your reality.

Often, we do things because it's what we're "supposed to do." We think we're exercising freedom of choice. Society conditions us to receive applause when we do "good" and criticism when we do "bad." In reality, there is no good or bad. There just is.

When we lose ourselves in duality—the idea that everything is its own individual subject and separate from everything else—we compare, segregate, and compartmentalize people, things, and events into their own category, limiting the perspectives we can have of them. Instead of seeing an event for what it is and without bias, we see an event as the media portrays it. Instead of seeing someone for who they are, we judge them through a lens of gossip or rumors. Instead of seeing the massive potential of a project, we label it for the early criticism it receives. Dual thinking creates room for comparison between what isn't instead of connection to what is.

Everything we deem as "correct" or "wrong" is one hundred percent subjective. There are no hard rules in the Universe. We are the creators of our own laws. The authority we give to the media and to social hierarchies like teachers, parents, and politicians is a crutch we lean upon to avoid being responsible for our choices and our reality. Everything they say, we consider true. But when we make a choice based on what others say and it doesn't work out for us, we're quick to point fingers and assign blame.

Social hierarchies have their benefits. Many times, they are useful. As a child, it's helpful to have your parents and teachers be guiding hands to introduce you to the world. As a sick patient, it's helpful to have someone with years of medical experience to give you advice. But just like your RAS (Reticular Activating System), if you take this to the extreme, there are negative side effects. A child who doesn't learn to think for himself becomes an adult incapable of making decisions. A sick patient who doesn't learn how to care for herself will be dependent forever on the pharmaceutical industry. The more we outsource our responsibility to others, the more sheep-like we become.

When we were kids, our parents trained us to follow authority. Over time, this turned into a habit. The problem? We were never untrained. There's no curriculum in place to teach us how to think for ourselves. To think creatively, we must think independently. The powers that be, like governments and large corporations, don't want independent thinkers, they want followers. If we're lucky, our parents taught us independence. If they didn't, we learned it ourselves through trial and error. Those who do not find their independence will be drowned by the noise. They will follow authority blindly and never connect with their inner truth.

Jordan followed the system. Growing up in a lower-middle-class family, his parents dreamed he'd rise above their station in life. He was smart, and his teachers encouraged college. But Jordan always wanted to be a drummer in a band—and he was a great one. Still, he craved the big house and nice car he saw in TV ads, and he didn't want to disappoint his family, so he chose dentistry. "Dentists make good money," his parents said.

After years of study, he graduated from a top university, burdened with massive student loans. He completed internships, passed every hurdle, and finally started practicing. The first few years flew by, and the money was decent. But one day, sitting in his office, he thought, "Do I really want to be a dentist?"

The answer didn't matter. He was deep in debt, with over a decade of effort sacrificed for this career, and the money was too comfortable to walk away. The "sunk cost fallacy" gripped him— the tendency to stick with something we've invested in, even if the costs now outweigh the benefits. That's when the realization hit him like a slap from the Universe: he'd been seduced by the noise.

The Outside Voices

We hold ourselves back from becoming who we were born to be because of outside voices. When we're born, we're born with a self—a personality, gift, talent, or way of being that's unique and authentic. Contrary to popular belief, our special gifts aren't developed from our environment, family, and friends. They come with the package that is us. The goal is not to shape ourselves into someone we think we're supposed to be, but to discover who we already are.

Since we're biological beings, the tendency to adopt characteristics from our cultural environment—creating a sense of safety and belonging—is wired into us through a process called *osmosis*. This process is also known as the ego. As the ego strengthens, we become increasingly absorbed in the illusion of who we think we are, limiting our ability to tap into our full creative potential. In this section, we'll explore the symptoms of a strong ego and how to address each one. But before we dive in, let me ask you a question.

Why do you want to create?

Are you creating for money, status, and recognition? Or is it for the love of the game? It's easy to get swept into ego-driven desires when we see teenagers becoming celebrities on TikTok, music producers climbing the charts, and "simple" art selling for millions. The allure of outcomes is potent. But in the process, we often lose sight of why we started creating in the first place—to discover ourselves, follow our calling, and connect with a higher Intelligence. What begins as a genuine, soul-driven pursuit can become a tool for the ego's gratification. Chasing these ego-based desires is a losing game, even when you win. You may spend years pursuing a goal that brings little joy or fulfillment. In today's increasingly transparent world, "faking it to make it" is harder than ever. If you follow your ego, you're likely to encounter the following symptoms:

◊ Perfectionism

A true creator understands the value of *finished imperfection*. To avoid criticism or rejection, perfectionists fail to publish, post, release, or end a project that required extensive amounts of their time, energy, and money. Imagine, for example, spending years writing a book. Then, you publish, and nobody likes it—this is the perfectionist's biggest fear.

Perfectionism can trap creatives in cycles of doubt, insecurity, and fear of judgment. But by embracing finished imperfection, you open yourself up to share your work with the world. This courage invites feedback from the Universe, sparking growth and evolution in your craft. When you stop holding onto others' opinions so tightly, perfectionism fades. Instead, your excitement propels you forward, allowing you to move on to the next project with newfound momentum, rather than being endlessly tethered to the same one.

Keep in mind, the "you" working on your project today won't be the same "you" working on it tomorrow. Time changes us, reshaping our inspirations and desires. Rather than constantly shifting focus or clinging to one project without evidence it's worthwhile, finish what you start. Each completed project builds your portfolio and gives you valuable insight. The only way to know if something is worth continuing or refining is to put it out for the world to see. Without sharing it, you'll never know. There's immense value in finishing and moving forward.

In traditional Japanese aesthetics, there is a philosophy called wabi-sabi (侘び寂び), which is centered on the acceptance of transience and imperfection. Nature is always changing and evolving, so nothing we create will ever remain static. It'll always be built upon, either by us or by future generations. By acknowledging the impermanence of everything we create, we're more likely to see the "reality of reality" and appreciate the work we do and the impact it has instead of judging ourselves for not reaching elusive or unattainable standards.

Imperfection is attractive and relatable. The bonsai tree, for example, is filled with gnarly twirls and curves, but it radiates character and charm. Organic fruits and vegetables may come in irregular colors and shapes, and have imperfections, but they taste delicious. Vintage clothing may be ripped or weathered, but it still has style, and when you wear it, you exude confidence. The quirkiness of someone's tattoos, the loudness of their laugh, or the unconventional style of their hair may be strange—but all their imperfections make them attractive. This is easy to see and say, but not always easy to believe and apply.

A perfectionist is highly self-critical, judging themselves harshly for not meeting certain standards. Often, these standards—set by outside voices like parents, teachers, or society—trap perfectionists in a loop of self-deprecating talk that erodes their self-esteem. Not getting it right the first time becomes reason enough to tear themselves down, hoping this will somehow build them up. Unfortunately, it does the opposite. To break this cycle, start by lowering your standards and valuing progress over perfection. Recognize the significance of small actions and successes, and consistently reinforce the value of taking steady steps toward your goals. When each step becomes a reason for celebration, you embody the mindset of a winner, not a critic.

While perfectionism has its downsides, it also has an upside. Being obsessive about your craft and aiming to excel isn't necessarily a bad thing. It's okay to push your creative limits to maximize impact and quality. Asking, "Is this the best I can do?" can lead to small refinements and tweaks that make a big difference.

If it doesn't feel right in your gut, don't settle. Insist until it feels complete. Until it feels yours. Do your absolute best with the knowledge base you have. Squeeze every ounce of present moment potential. Once you're satisfied, let go, and move onto the next project. There's a fine line between making simple tweaks and falling into perfectionism. To avoid crossing it, try focusing on iteration instead.

Perfectionism

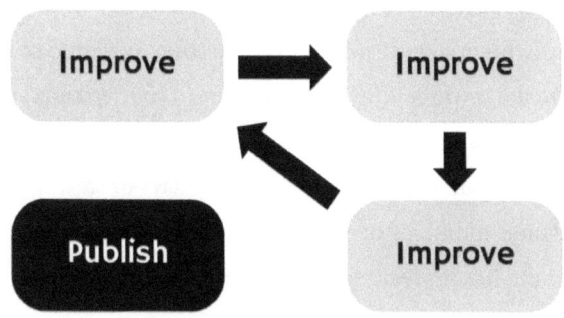

Iteration

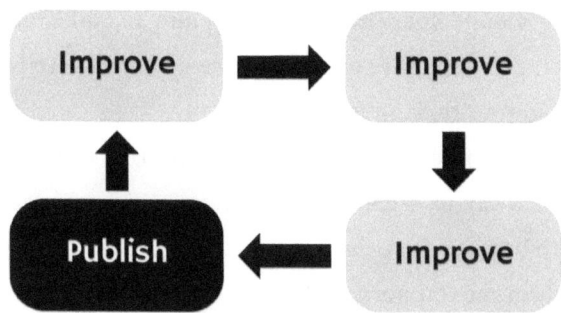

Iteration follows a four-step process: create, finish, improve, then repeat. Perfectionism skips the "finish" step. While it urges you to improve, it keeps you stuck. Iteration, on the other hand, lets you keep moving while constantly improving. If something is ninety percent good, it's good enough—the last ten percent is often an illusion. Trying to hit 100 percent can strip your work of authenticity, and over-editing removes the unique nuances that make it yours. Moving on preserves your essence and helps you produce more quickly. This approach is how I finish and publish a book within thirty to ninety days of starting it. Once I've made the most of my perfectionist drive, I move on and apply the lessons learned to the next project.

◊ Imposter Syndrome

If you spent your entire life being someone you're not, the idea of reverting to your essence might seem freeing, but in reality, it's terrifying. You've built a life around who you thought you were—around your "mask." Shifting into an authentic version of you can feel you're dismantling everything you've built and turning your back on it.

On the surface, living behind a mask is easy. It provides a buffer, a way to distance yourself from criticism, rejection, or failure because the person experiencing it isn't truly you—it's the character you portray. The real fear comes from embracing your authentic self and being open to the same scrutiny. Now, it's no longer the mask they're criticizing. It's you.

Mask

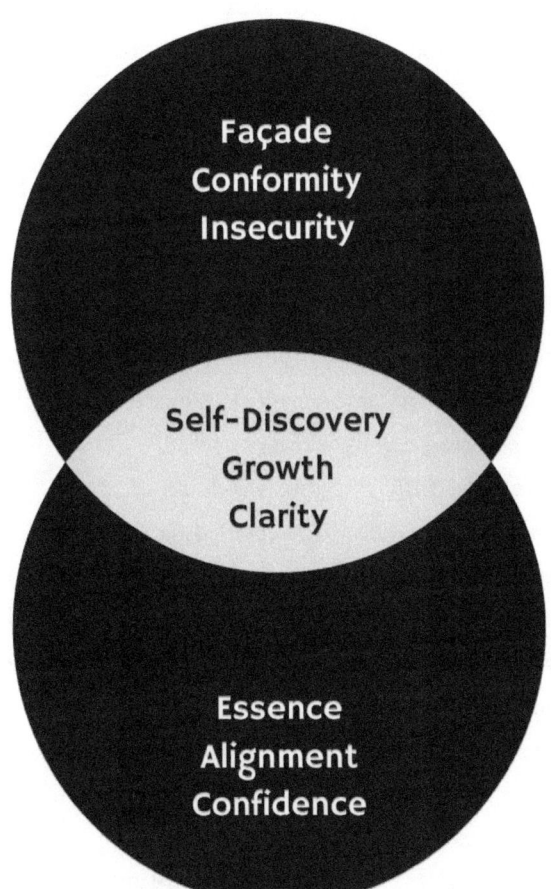

Façade
Conformity
Insecurity

Self-Discovery
Growth
Clarity

Essence
Alignment
Confidence

Authentic Self

Imposter syndrome is the inability to believe that you deserve or are worthy of success. Therefore, you wear a mask, protecting yourself from revealing your authentic self. When you succeed while wearing the mask, the success feels undeserved, as though the character you portray is the one who achieved it—not the real you. You question whether you, at your core, are capable of the same success without the mask.

The deeper fear of imposter syndrome is that if you allow yourself to be authentic—if you step into your truth—failure or judgment will cut much deeper. Authenticity makes you vulnerable. The fear is no longer about whether you can handle the success; it's about whether your authentic self can stand up to the challenges that come with it. This makes stepping into your power feel like a daunting risk.

Here's the truth. Fear and self-doubt are good. They show you the way. The more frightened you are of your calling, the more sure you can be that you have to do it. Your greatest feats will come off the back of your biggest fears. The ideas that spark emotion and motivation in others will come when you're at your most vulnerable. There's a direct correlation between openness and the ability to channel ideas. The more open you are to becoming who you're meant to be, the more abundance you can create and attract.

The feeling of imposter syndrome will always be there. You just get better at managing it. There's no such thing as a fearless actor stepping onto the stage. They just learn to use the fear to their advantage. Embrace this as part of the journey and keep going.

◊ Victimhood

Responsibility requires owning up to your choices and mistakes. For the ego, this is bad news, because it diminishes your status and rank within your social circle. To avoid this, the ego often adopts a victim mindset—casting you as someone at the mercy of external forces. The ego blames your parents, the economy, or life circumstances for holding you back from manifesting your dreams. But barriers to your creativity cannot be removed when you're busy pointing fingers. By deflecting focus from yourself, you're self-sabotaging your progress. Taking responsibility for your actions is the key to true progress and success.

To avoid taking ownership of our lives, we often create self-imposed limitations that manifest in various ways. Health is one of the most common. Those who resist responsibility may subconsciously attract health issues, using physical incapacitation as an excuse for inaction. To soothe our pain, we seek sympathy, and others' validation only reinforces our victim mindset, affirming a sense of helplessness rather than empowerment.

I like to think of creativity or the act of creating as a sport. Athletes obsessed with winning will do everything they can to be ready and fit for game day. The victim? They'll eat junk food, avoid exercise, and hope that something happens so they can avoid the work.

But even with a serious health condition or disability, you still have choice. To play the victim or the creator. To take responsibility every day to improve and take steps toward your dream, or to sit back moaning about why the world is unfair. Nick Vujicic, a motivational speaker, author, and father, is the perfect example of someone who was a creator instead of a victim.

Born without arms and legs, Nick endured years of bullying, depression, and even suicidal thoughts during his younger years. He found strength in his faith, family, and desire to inspire others facing their own struggles. Despite his physical limitations, he trained himself to perform tasks such as writing, typing, swimming, and even surfing! At nineteen, he began giving speeches and was invited to travel the world, delivering powerful talks and inspiring millions of people. Eventually, he wrote his own book.

People like Nick Vujicic are rare. However, Nick is a perfect representation of making an empowering choice—living out what he was destined to do, instead of succumbing to pressure and judgment from outside voices.

Victimhood can also lead to self-dramatization. We'll dramatize everything in our lives if it means pulling attention from what we're supposed to be doing. When everything is important, nothing gets done. Drama will fill your mind with useless information and drain you of valuable energy. The ego loves it. Drama is like a black-hole, sucking up everybody's vital life force for the sake of entertainment. It prevents people from doing the uncomfortable thing—stepping into the greatest version of who they can be.

When there's no health problem or drama to soak up attention, a victim will revert to blaming unseen forces, like luck or fate, for their lack of success. Statements like "I'm not lucky like other people" or "It's just not meant to be" frequent a victim's mind. They live as if they are cursed, and by doing so, they create that reality for themselves—a self-fulfilling prophecy. Nothing works out. The timing is never right. They can never catch a break. The victim will manifest their own struggle to avoid being who they are.

But underneath these avoidance tactics lies the number one fear that entrenches our minds. This fear is the root of limitation. It connects and entangles every other fear you can name—the fear of success.

◊ The Fear of Success

The fear of success is like spending days climbing to the top of a mountain, only to stop just before the peak because you're afraid of heights. You've done all the work, but you hesitate to step onto the summit because of what you'll see (or what you'll realize about yourself). Being at the top means confronting new challenges, increased expectations, and the unknown. It means stepping into a role that demands more of us, and sometimes, we fear that the success we've worked for will require us to leave behind the comfort of what we know.

The higher you go up the mountain, the bigger the drop. Instead of focusing on our accomplishments and potential, we focus on what we'll lose if we fail. If we were ever to fall from grace, we'd hate to see the looks on the faces of those we love. We're afraid of what happens because of success, not the success itself. The people we might lose. The responsibilities that might pile up. The purpose that might fade. What happens after we reach the finish line?

This is what people get choked up about. But there is no finish line. There is no end to all of this. Success is just a stepping-stone for the next goal, for the next desire. Success can be what brings you the resources to make the impact you've always wanted to make or to have the freedom to choose a fresh path.

We have a craving for infinity. Allow yourself to fulfill this craving by beginning a journey that you never want to end. Allow success to be a part of that journey. This is the most creative—and the quietest—path.

The sounds of limitation are all around us. The purpose of this chapter was to shine a light on patterns potentially holding you back from stepping into your most creative self. When we know our blocks, we gain the ability to move forward with clarity and purpose. However, clarity is only half the battle.

Now that you've identified the symptoms and patterns rooted in the ego—perfectionism, imposter syndrome, victimhood, and fear of success—you have the power to dismantle them. Awareness opens the door, but action propels you to new heights. Remember, true creativity thrives not in perfection or control, but in flow, trust, and surrender. The following chapters will provide guidance to silence these blocks so you can embrace the full spectrum of your creative potential.

Summary for Chapter 3: The Sound of Limitation
Law #3: Noise Clouds Creativity

- **Defining Noise:** Noise includes societal expectations, external judgments, and false desires others implant that derail you from your truth.

- **Outside Voices are Loud:** Social media and societal norms shape your thoughts and reality without you realizing it—they're more persuasive than we think.

- **Duality and Comparison:** Dualistic thinking leads to unnecessary comparisons and limits creativity by segmenting life into "good" or "bad."

- **Perfectionism:** Perfectionism stifles progress. Accept finished imperfection, embrace the process of iteration, and move forward to the next project.

- **Imposter Syndrome:** Feeling unworthy of success or fearing judgment holds your authentic self back from shining. However, it also shows you the way. Your greatest feats will come off the back of your biggest fears.

- **Victimhood:** Blaming external forces, circumstances, or bad luck keeps you from owning your creative potential. Take responsibility and move forward.

- **Fear of Success:** The fear of what happens after success can cause self-sabotage. Embrace success as a part of the journey rather than a finish line.

Journaling Prompts

- **Identifying Noise:** What external opinions or societal expectations shape your decisions and perspectives? How have they influenced your creative process?

Exercises

- **Digital Detox:** Spend one full day disconnected from social media, news, and other external influences. During this time, journal about the thoughts, ideas, and emotions that arise in the absence of external noise.

- **Imposter Syndrome Challenge:** Write down three accomplishments you're proud of and reflect on how your authentic self contributed to each one. Acknowledge your worth and capability in achieving success.

- **Perfectionism Breakthrough:** Choose a creative project you've been stuck on because of perfectionism. Set a deadline for completion and commit to finishing and sharing it, even if it feels imperfect.

CHAPTER 4

Become Soundproof

❖

LAW #4:

Silence Opens Channels

The quieter you become, the more you can hear.
— **Ram Dass**

D uring the quietest moments of my life, I am at my most creative. Funny how this works. We often correlate creativity with a bombastic, extroverted personality. After all, a big part of creativity is surrounding ourselves with sources of inspiration. Try writing a book without ever having read one. Try painting a landscape without ever having gone for a hike. Try composing a song without having listened to music. Art is infinitely more difficult to create when you have had no exposure to art. However, I've realized there is a fine line between surrounding yourself with "inspiration" and surrounding yourself with "noise." This line is more blurry than most people realize.

Throughout the production of my first six books, I didn't feel called to explore. Travel, adventures, and social events weren't a significant part of my lifestyle like they are today. My priority was to complete the series, which I'd planned out in 2019. I published book number six in 2022. My only reasons for exposing myself to noise were to visit family, attend mastermind events, or change the scenery.

I didn't explore the world then like I do today because those books were my world. Every ounce of my energy was going toward creating work that was innovative, engaging, and valuable to the reader—no easy feat, especially since when I started, I had no experience. Hundreds of thousands of books on philosophy, metaphysics, and Universal laws are out there, but few stand out from the crowd. I needed to take extreme measures to compensate for my lack of experience. To maximize my creativity and energy, I isolated myself so I could hear the whispers of my soul. I knew if I was going to create something substantial; it needed to come from within.

We've conditioned ourselves to see reality as being material. But reality is spiritual. When you master the spiritual realm, you master the physical realm. The less noise we have occupying our mental, emotional, and physical space, the more we hear our intuition. Intuition is a subtle impulse to do something expansive. It's your soul guiding you in the direction of your highest excitement and passion. Often, when you listen to your intuition, it goes against all the noise you've been hearing. By finding silence in your day-to-day, you become capable of listening to the quiet beat of your intuition.

Planned isolation can lead to elevated states of creativity and flow. When there is no noise drowning out the impulses of your heart, your inner genius flourishes, and you can birth ideas that resonate and leave a lasting impact.

Seek Silence

Beneath the noise, there is silence. Silence is the bedrock of reality. Noise can't exist without silence, just like music can't exist without sound and thoughts can't exist without mind. There are different layers to existence, and when you notice the silence, you notice reality and bring awareness to the truth.

By seeking silence in our everyday lives, we tune in to the deepest, most authentic layer of our perception. That layer isn't biased, conditioned, or clouded with outside noise. The more you accustom yourself to silence, the closer you get to experiencing the purest version of reality. This is why yogis and monks meditate—to seek silence and connect with truth.

In meditation, you're blocking out noise. When applied inwardly, it's self-inquiry. When applied outwardly, it's observation. These practices happen without judgment. Judgment comes from the ego. Judgment is noise. Without judgment, there is silence and you can hear your soul's whisper. Your inner genius can pitch in, and your inspiration can shine through. Living in silence is the ultimate state for channeling creativity.

In this section, we're going to discuss three practical ways of seeking silence and tapping into its power—solitude, stillness, and speed. For the sake of memorization, we'll call them the Three S's of Silence.

◊ Solitude

We live in a hyper-connected world. We can send messages, take calls, and have video chats with people from across the seven continents in real time. Despite this, we're lonelier than ever. The issue isn't a lack of people who share our interests and values; it's that our connections are clouded by noise. Our interactions are filtered through digital images, follower counts, and text exchanges, where genuine friendships morph into networking groups and romantic partners become status symbols. Egos bond with egos, and in the process, we're losing touch with what it means to truly connect.

Because of our hyper-connectivity, solitude is demonized. Outside noise conditions us to fear spending time alone. Fear of missing out and judgment are pushing us to seek solace in others. Over time, our sense of self as individuals dissipates, and our identities become dependent on the presence and approval of others. In our desperation to find and maintain our "tribe," we soften our boundaries, fill every gap in our calendar with social events, and never spend time with ourselves.

The world is headed into a technological age. There's no avoiding it. It's imperative that we don't lose ourselves in this tide of advancements.

A few months ago, a friend and I traveled to Japan for the first time. Almost immediately, something caught my eye. In nearly every cafe, restaurant, or bar we went into, there were many people sitting alone. A local deli had twelve to fifteen customers, and *everyone was sitting alone*. People were reading, studying, eating, watching videos, or simply being. The silence was soothing. It turns out there is a cultural movement in Japan known as *solo katsu* (ソロ活), the concept of finding time to spend with oneself—doing activities or attending venues that are (or were) tailored toward groups.

Within Japanese culture, there's a long-standing value of putting others' needs before one's own. Paired with external pressures and expectations, the constant connectivity of the modern world can feel suffocating. Solo katsu provides an oasis—a chance to recenter and find peace in a world that's always demanding our attention.

Dr. Maya Angelou's approach to writing beautifully illustrates the power of solitude in the creative process. By retreating to a quiet, bare hotel room, she left behind the distractions and expectations of daily life, creating a space solely for her thoughts and words. In solitude, she tapped into a unique clarity. The type of clarity you can't discover when you're bombarded with opinions, judgements, and egos. This allowed her to be vulnerable with her work and free with her ideas. Her practice is a reminder that true creativity often requires stepping away from the noise of the world—into spaces of solitude—where we can fully connect with our deepest, most authentic selves.

When applying the principle of solitude, it's important that you don't get demanding or defensive about your alone time. Solitude is not about isolating yourself from the world like a hermit. It's about discovering who you are so you can engage with the world authentically. In solitude, you're more likely to catch the thinking patterns, tendencies, and bad habits that limit the way you show up in the world.

This is why I'm such a big fan of solo travel. When you travel solo, you proactively put yourself in a position to explore and engage with the world as an individual versus as part of a group. By immersing yourself in new cultures, groups, and activities by yourself, you're expanding your perception of what it means to be you. New thoughts arise and you're inspired to act because there's no conditioning holding you back. Contrary to what you might think, there's more adventure in solitude than meets the eye.

◇ Stillness

The demands and volatility of today's economy have pushed many of us to overextend in our work and projects. Setting a clear intention when pursuing a goal is invaluable—it brings focus and direction, and most people could benefit from this advice. Yet, for those who lean to the opposite end of the spectrum—the ones who don't pause, who rest too little—the advice needs to be tailored. They require guidance in setting intentional boundaries for rest and renewal, knowing when to pause, and recognizing that clarity often emerges from moments of stillness, not endless striving.

Overworking has led to a rise in burnout and health conditions we've never seen in modern times. The constant rush to get things done, meet deadlines, and prove ourselves has led to more problems than we'd like to admit. Studies have shown a significant increase in stress-related illnesses such as heart disease, anxiety, and depression. According to the World Health Organization, burnout is now recognized as a medical condition linked directly to the demands, conditions, and stresses of the workplace. We've also discovered that productivity and creativity does not necessarily improve with longer hours—in fact, chronic overworking has been found to reduce efficiency, further exacerbating the problem.

Countless events are categorized as "once in a lifetime opportunities." But little do we realize, these "rare events" come and go every year. Sure, there are a few opportunities that are bigger and gain more media attention than others, but if you pay attention, these so-called life-changing opportunities are everywhere always. Depending on the person acting on them, they can either be noise that distracts you or a chance to carry out your purpose. Connecting to silence and knowing who you are will bring clarity to this decision and help you make the right one at the right time.

Don't let the fear of missing out condition you to rush through life. Rushing puts you in a state of desperation and worry, making you more likely to stumble. When you hurry, you push your desires further away. Progress comes from steady, intentional effort.

To slow down, give yourself permission to simply be. Sometimes, the most productive choice is to do *nothing*. Forcing a project that doesn't need it often does more harm than good. Let the Universe arrange the pieces—it possesses a wisdom and power beyond comprehension. Each day, subtle events align to support your journey, even if you're unaware of them. Clarity emerges when you allow yourself the gift of stillness.

◊ Speed

Almost two years ago, a friend wanted to prove to himself that with enough action, focus, and intention, anybody can overcome their self-doubt to start an online business. He challenged himself to create a Shopify store (something he'd never done before) and sell an online product over the weekend. Within three days, his store was live, running ads, and selling units of a magnetic phone mount. It wasn't much, but it was enough to spark him with inspiration and evidence that he (or anybody), can be an entrepreneur. Speed of execution is the solution for a doubtful mind.

The reason many of us struggle with doubt is not because of past traumas or external factors. It's because we're too slow to act on inspiration. We ponder everything, which leaves room for the ego to latch onto our thoughts, clouding them with fear and limitation. Many of your negative thoughts would go away if you just acted faster on the projects you thought of or if you produced the art you felt inspired to create. This is not the same as being in a rush. Being in a rush is fear of missing the train. You're thinking about what you might miss as opposed to what there is to gain. Speed is about being quick to experiment, test, and move forward with your next decision.

If you're quick to act, the worst-case scenario is that you'll fail and learn something. This is better than the opposite—succumbing and accepting the arguments of the ego. If you surrender to the ego enough times, you'll condition yourself to make decisions in a state of limitation rather than possibility.

When falling victim to doubts becomes a habit, your doubts compound into beliefs, cementing themselves deeper into your subconscious mind. The faster you can catch these doubts and act despite your fear, the quicker you can untangle yourself from the webs of your ego.

How quickly you act on impulse and inspiration reflects your commitment to your dreams and trust in the Universe. There's a time and place to think and ponder, but there's also a time and place to act, regardless of any ego argument. If you feel in your soul you want and need to do something, do it. Forget about the outcome. Move so fast you don't give your ego time to come up with excuses because it's too busy processing the new data you're throwing at it. Shock your system with speed. Submerge yourself in the unknown. Allow instinct and intuition to be your guides.

In 1984, Richard Branson was on vacation in the British Virgin Islands when his flight to Puerto Rico was canceled. Instead of waiting around and feeling frustrated, he took matters into his own hands. He thought, "What if there were another way?" Before his mind could conjure up doubts and assumptions, he went back to the airport, hired a private plane, found a chalkboard left unattended by another airline, and wrote, "Virgin Airways: $39.00 single flight to Puerto Rico." Soon he had filled the plane with enough passengers to cover the cost of the flight. This spontaneous and quick-witted decision led to the idea for Virgin Airways. A decisive mind is a doubtless mind.

The quicker you move, the less unmade decisions are taking up space in your mind. When your actions are inspiring, your thoughts follow. Allow yourself to follow your intuition full-heartedly. Don't wait for conditions to be perfect or for the validation of others. If it doesn't work out, it doesn't work out. Move on to the next thing. Your intuition is never wrong. It'll always guide you to the highest lesson or experience that's possible for you at every moment.

Become soundproof. The more silence you have in your life, the more connected you are to Spirit. This is when you'll find all of your best ideas—the moment your mind is blank. Like when you're taking a shower. Right before you fall asleep. During an evening walk in nature. Ideas come where there is space for them to appear.

Summary for Chapter 4: Become Soundproof
Law #4: Silence Opens Channels to Inspiration

- **The Power of Silence:** Creativity thrives in quiet moments. Noise often distracts us from our intuition, limiting our potential to tap into creativity.

- **Noise versus Inspiration:** Inspiration is essential, but too much external noise clouds your mind with labels, assumptions, and doubts. Silence allows us to differentiate between genuine creativity and the noise of others' expectations.

- **Planned Isolation:** By seeking solitude and silence intentionally, we become more connected to our intuition and capable of producing creative and authentic work.

- **Seek Solitude, Stillness, and Speed:** These three practices open channels for creativity by silencing the noise and focusing the mind on what truly matters.

- **Solitude as a Tool:** Solitude isn't about isolating oneself; it's about discovering one's true self and understanding how to engage with the world authentically.

- **The Importance of Stillness:** Taking time to slow down and reflect allows the Universe to guide you in ways you can't imagine if you're constantly rushing.

- **The Power of Speed:** Acting quickly on inspiration prevents self-doubt and allows you to stay ahead of the noise, reinforcing trust in your intuition.

Journaling Prompts

- **Quiet the Noise:** Reflect on areas of your life where external noise (such as social media, expectations, or judgments) is silencing your inner voice. What actions can you take to create more silence and space for your creativity to flourish?

- **Solitude Exploration:** How do you feel when you're alone? Is it uncomfortable or peaceful? How might spending more time in solitude help you connect with your true desires and intuition?

- **Speed of Action:** Think of a time when you acted quickly on inspiration. What was the outcome? How did acting fast affect your confidence and creativity?

Exercises

- **Solo Activity Challenge:** Dedicate a day to doing something alone you'd normally do with others—like dining out, going to a movie, or taking a trip. Write down your thoughts and insights after the experience.

- **Create Stillness:** Incorporate a daily practice of stillness—whether it's ten minutes of meditation, journaling in silence, or simply sitting without distraction. After a week, reflect on any shifts in your creativity or mental clarity.

- **Speed Exercise:** The next time you feel inspired, act on it immediately. Write down the results of this quick action, regardless of the outcome, and reflect on how it felt to move fast without overthinking.

CHAPTER 5

The Art of Seeing

LAW #5:

Unique Perceptions Trigger Innovation

The eye sees only what the mind is prepared to comprehend.
— **Henri Bergson**

Innovation shapes our world, enhancing our experience of reality through groundbreaking creations. It is the highest expression of creative energy, the driving force that shifts paradigms and makes what once seemed impossible, possible. To step into the role of an innovative thinker, you must cultivate *lateral thinking*—embracing unconventional perspectives and breaking out of traditional mental frameworks. This requires knowing how to perceive reality differently from the norm. To create something original is a powerful way of changing the world. We're not here to replicate or imitate. We're here to create what doesn't yet exist and to elevate art, businesses, products, and services to new levels.

History's greatest innovators never followed the norm. When Thomas Edison created the light bulb, for example, it wasn't just a triumph in technology, but an expression of his relentless pursuit to bring light into a dark world, making over 1,000 failed attempts before cracking the code. When Steve Jobs introduced the first iPhone, it wasn't just a gadget. It reflected his vision of revolutionizing the way we connect. Innovation is the authentic expression of our deepest excitement, passion, and calling. But it's also a reflection of elevated levels of thinking that transcend the obvious and predictable.

Innovation doesn't happen by just jumping on trends or recycling old ideas. It's about seeing things differently, taking what's uniquely yours, and letting it reshape the way we think and live. When you tap into your individuality and creativity, that's when the magic happens—you're not just standing out; you're setting the stage for something genuinely new. There is a creative force inside every one of us, but for many people, it's bottled up. This creative force, like a magnet, can attract and influence large-scale audiences, global companies, or even just our local groups, families, or communities. The more authentic and diverse we are with our thinking, the more innovative we become in our everyday lives.

Innovative thinking gives us the opportunity to bring spice and color to a world that's dull and grey. When we stop chasing what's already been done and start trusting our own creative voice, we become a one-of-a-kind force of innovation.

Perceive Beyond Expectation

The world is louder when we're judgmental. Our ego, like a spider spinning its web, instantly labels and defines reality, weaving a network of narratives that feel logical and orderly. In nature, the spider starts with anchor strands, setting a framework, then adds layers until it forms the capture spiral at the center—the final but essential piece. Similarly, our ego acts as the "capture spiral" in our mental web. It's the last part constructed but becomes the purpose behind the entire web. This web of judgment and categorization helps us make sense of our experiences, deciding what feels safe and what doesn't.

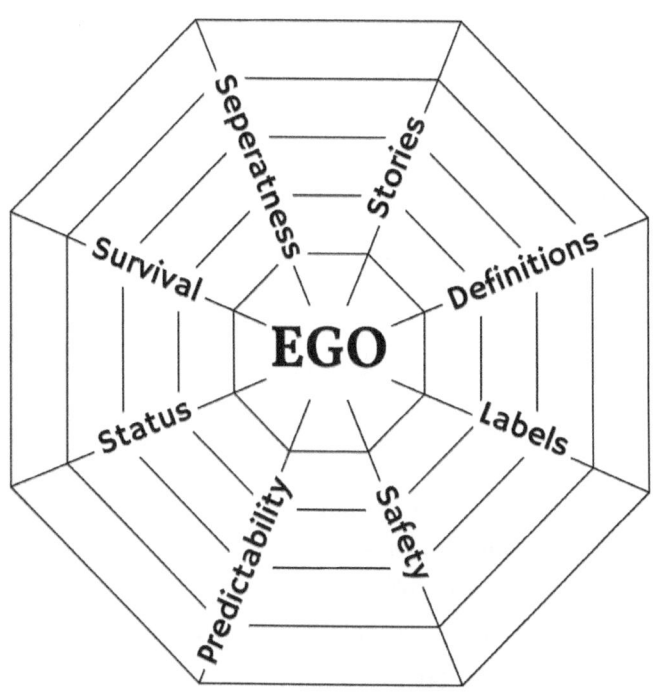

By judging the world, we limit our potential experiences based on our assumptions, biases, and beliefs. When we judge with labels, we narrow our perception. Instead of seeing things for what they are, we see them through the lens of our conditioning. The RAS (Reticular Activating System) goes to work to filter our experience, putting us in a constant search for evidence and proof that confirms our existing beliefs. When we narrow our perception, we narrow our creativity.

The skill of seeing is an unfiltered awareness of reality. Leonardo da Vinci called this strategy of thinking *saper veder*, which means "knowing how to see." It's about observing reality without judgment—engaging with a neutral, authentic perception, so you see the truth of what *is* (as opposed to the illusion you're conditioned to seek). While the ego feels lack wherever it goes, the Spirit observes, knowing it's one with the abundance all around us. The ego lives through memories and traumas while the Spirit lives through truth and potential. The better you get at seeing, the more aligned you are with Spirit, the more possibilities you access, and the deeper insights you gain.

We cannot see more than we expect to see. By experiencing reality with labels and stereotypes, we cannot see beyond our biases and preconceived notions. Our expectations create our reality. But they can also blind us of blessings.

An example of this is when Banksy, a famous British street artist, set up a stall in Central Park selling original signed copies of his work as part of a social experiment. Typically, his art pieces would sell for hundreds of thousands of dollars each, but he sold each one for around $60. Unaware of its true value, few people took notice and only a handful purchased his art. One person even tried to haggle! This experiment highlighted just how much context influences people's perception of value and creativity. This happens often throughout our day.

For example, we might reject ideas from friends and family based on our experiences with and assumptions about the person. We might reject a business or product based on our first impression or on how it was presented. We often define value based on superficial judgments like price, status, or location. Throughout your life's journey, you might be required not only to challenge your own assumptions but also to challenge assumptions of others. The art of seeing is about being able to recognize the true value that something holds, while also considering the context in which it's being presented. We often lose ourselves in the negative because we're conditioned for it—this is known as negativity bias.

The art of seeing enhances your ability to think positive thoughts and have an optimistic outlook. When you can't see the light at the end of the tunnel, you need to find a different path. This often requires creative thinking. One of the biggest reasons people cannot master the laws of manifestation is because they're unable to think creatively in order to perceive beyond the negative. Seeing is a skill. When you develop this skill, the positive side of any situation becomes easier to find and focus on.

In the following pages, we'll be discussing various techniques for stretching your imagination and allowing you to expand the scope of your perception so you can see things that most people do not see. In doing so, you'll gain the ability to connect with sources of inspiration and ideas that can change the reality of your mind, project, problem, or situation.

Re-sensitization

One of the simplest ways of connecting with different dimensions of reality is by re-sensitizing our senses. Over the past two decades, we've become exposed to a barrage of stimulants. Constant noise, artificial lights, and synthetic textures have dulled our natural perception, making ordinary experiences less meaningful. The more we consume, the more we need to consume to achieve the same effects—like the person who needs more wine to feel the same buzz. This desensitization process isn't limited to substances. It applies to everything in life.

Our relationships suffer because we find people around us boring when we compare them to the endless streams of dopamine-spiking entertainment at our fingertips. Genuine connections require us to be present, but our minds have been conditioned to seek novelty. Even the foods we eat are showered in chemicals that hook us, keeping us wanting more. We've overpowered our natural taste buds and have disconnected from the flavors of real, unprocessed ingredients.

By developing sensory awareness, we become more sensitive to the world. We begin to re-sensitize ourselves to the people, foods, and information that bring us health, joy, and fulfillment. At healthy doses, everything we taste, hear, touch, smell, and feel brings a more enriching experience. The art of seeing is about paying attention to what comes into contact with our senses—the music we listen to, the foods we eat, the people we hang around, and the information we consume.

The world has so much to offer. Our modern tendency is to demand more from it, which keeps us ignorant and unaware of the abundance that's already there. More material doesn't mean more value. Learn to detox from stimulants like your phone, the internet, and sugary foods and reconnect with the natural state of your senses.

You can discover more by embracing less. Beneath the surface of everyday people, places, and objects lies a depth of information, inspiration, and wisdom that many overlook. When you cut down on distractions that drain your energy, you open yourself to more inspiration, become sensitive to the subtle details of the present, and start welcoming ideas that resonate with your authentic self.

Adjust Your Distance

Another way of stretching your perception of an idea, experience, or problem is by learning to zoom in and zoom out. By adjusting the distance through which you perceive a subject, you gain access to multiple different layers of perception. Looking at the stars with your eyes is a completely different experience than looking at them through a telescope. Similarly, observing an ant from a standing position offers a general view of its movement, yet looking at it under a microscope reveals a complex world of structure and behavior. When you move closer or farther away from something, you perceive it in a whole new light.

When you're immersed in a project, it's easy to lose sight of the greater vision and fall victim to difficulties. Take a step back. See the big picture. Recognize how small these moments are compared to the timeline you're on. Notice how far you've come and how much more there still is to experience. By zooming out, you put less importance on today's challenges and successes, and remind yourself to appreciate each moment.

In the context of your long-term vision, one day will not make or break you. It is the compounded effect of your daily actions over months and years that will determine your fate. When it comes to creativity, you'll likely have days where you're channeling ideas left, right, and center, and you'll also have days with nothing.

Understand that innovative ideas can also come as a result of compounded thoughts and reflections. A breakthrough rarely happens on the first iteration of an idea. This is why there are beta-versions and prototypes. They are the beginning steps of an invention still in the developmental phase. When you zoom out, you prevent yourself from getting caught up in today's limitations and instead, you focus on tomorrow's possibilities.

If you find yourself overwhelmed with thoughts about the past and future, zoom in. Focus on the small steps. Bring yourself into the present moment. One of the true and tested ways to achieve a significant outcome is by compounding little daily actions for a long enough period. When you focus on doing the work today, you're one step closer to achieving your desired tomorrow. By zooming in, you purposefully narrow your perception to block out the noise from the outside. Not only does this help you focus, but it also brings attention to the nuances of reality.

When you take a closer look at something, you start noticing details that bring a fresh level of appreciation and insight. This shift in perspective can spark ideas you'd never see otherwise. Take Velcro, for example: Swiss engineer George de Mestral was out hiking when he noticed prickly seeds sticking to his dog's fur. Curious, he examined them under a microscope and found they had tiny hooks—an "aha" moment that led to the invention of Velcro.

By taking a closer look at what's often overlooked and zooming out on what's usually right in front of us, we open up a whole new lens through which to see the world. Investigate what most people ignore. Step back when most people are focused on details. It'll give you a whole new lens through which to see the world.

Perceptual Positions

A large part of how we see things comes from the position we find ourselves in relative to the subject. Imagine placing an object in the middle of a football stadium with an audience of 100,000. Each person in the crowd will have a different viewpoint of the object they're observing. As a result, each will form their unique impression, leading to different thoughts, emotions, or ideas.

A beginner will always have a different perspective than an expert. Looking at a problem with fresh eyes gives you the ability to see blind spots that others, who see the problem in traditional ways, might miss. An expert can point out problems or solutions that the beginner might not be aware of. Both positions have pros and cons, but by exploring both sides of the proverbial coin, you gain a deeper understanding of the coin as a whole.

If you want to change your perspective on a problem, learn to change the position from which you observe it. For example, often, during an argument, we can clash with another person because they are defending their position. To elevate the conversation, put yourself in the other person's shoes. By understanding their perspective, it's easier to find common ground.

Change your shoes. When you put yourself in someone else's shoes, you gain insight into what they're perceiving, and in turn, how they're thinking and feeling. You can also discover ideas and solutions that may have been invisible to you at first. Businesses often adopt the perspective of their customers to better understand their needs and desires, developing more effective marketing strategies as a result.

Another example is if you find yourself struggling to maintain a positive outlook on life. Gratitude might feel distant, and accepting things as they are could seem impossible. In such moments, try changing your position. Imagine yourself in the shoes of someone who has less than you—feel how they might think or experience life.Alternatively, take a trip back in time and reflect on your younger, less accomplished self. Look at how far you've come and how much you've achieved. We often fail to appreciate what we have until it's gone. This simple shift in perspective can unlock a deeper sense of gratitude and a renewed appreciation for where you are now.

When you limit yourself to one position, you limit yourself to one perspective—your own. Perceiving reality only from your position keeps you from learning from people in positions of greater abundance, freedom, or fulfillment. One of the most impactful teachings in manifestation books is the technique of *modeling*. By stepping into the shoes of someone you admire for their confidence, charisma, or success, you can tap into their energy field and access the vibration of their thoughts and emotions. You can also apply this to your future self.

By asking yourself, "What would the best future version of me do in this situation?" you're tuning into a higher energy. Often, we lack insight because of limitations stemming from our present mindset. To move past this, we must learn to project our consciousness into different "positions" within time and space. As you've likely noticed, these new positions aren't necessarily physical. The process of "changing your shoes" happens energetically. Shifting your position not only offers a new perspective—it can transform your energy and raise your vibration.

Surprising Connections

As I touched on earlier, everything is interconnected. But to make sense of the world, our minds often separate reality into neat categories. When someone crosses these lines, people might say things like, "stay in your lane" or "stick to what you know." This mindset limits creativity by boxing us into a narrow range of ideas. To escape this, we need to start making surprising connections—seeing links between things that, at first glance, don't seem related at all. It's these unusual correlations that open up new creative possibilities.

The process of discovering surprising connections involve grabbing ideas, concepts, and procedures from unrelated industries and applying them to your own with no preconceptions or prejudice.

By making these connections, you're able to see correlations that most people overlook simply because they "don't make sense." Here's the trick: everything makes sense if you find the sense in it.

For example, say you're coding a new app, but you're stuck on how to simplify the user interface. Instead of looking for solutions within traditional tech companies, draw inspiration from your local fast-food restaurant's menu. The creators of these menus design them for simplicity and speed, with a clear, visual flow that helps customers make quick decisions. By applying that same principle to your app, you might create a user interface that allows for quicker navigation. This type of cross-industry correlation—between fast food and tech—is unusual, but it allows you to think outside the box and generate innovative solutions.

Many of the ideas in my books and emails come from observing nature. I could watch a woodpecker pecking at a tree and come up with an email idea about persistence and consistency. I enjoy spending time at the beach, and every time I see the waves coming and going, I get the idea to talk about the cyclical nature of reality. Everything can be a source of inspiration if you give it the right meaning.

When we limit ourselves to the obvious, we'll only ever create what's obvious. Every day, obvious things are created and done. Innovation happens when you find obscure correlations. These ideas stretch your mind and allow you to see connections between things you've always known but never associated together.

A real-life example of this is when Steve Jobs drew inspiration for the design of the Apple retail stores from the hospitality industry, specifically high-end hotels. Jobs wanted the Apple Store to be more than just a place to buy products. He wanted it to be an experience. By focusing on customer service and atmosphere, much like luxury hotels do, he was able to create a space that was clean, inviting, and focused on the user experience. This correlation between the hospitality industry and retail electronics wasn't obvious, but it helped transform the way people shop for technology and contributed to Apple's success.

The art of seeing gives you the ability to be fluid and adaptable in our fast-changing, unpredictable world. When you can see beyond what most people notice, you're catching ideas fresh out of the "universal oven" and implementing them before others even realize their potential. The better you get at seeing past illusions, the faster you'll progress in the endeavors that ignite your passion.

Summary for Chapter 5: The Art of Seeing
Law #5: Unique Perceptions Trigger Innovative Ideas

- **Innovation and Lateral Thinking:** Innovation stems from perceiving reality differently. Lateral thinking breaks us free from conventional patterns, allowing us to bring new ideas into existence.

- **Perception Shapes Reality:** Our judgments, biases, and expectations limit our perceptions. By removing these filters, we open ourselves to a broader, more authentic view of reality.

- **Re-sensitization:** Because we are overstimulated, we've become desensitized to the world. By re-sensitizing ourselves, we reconnect with the richness of ordinary experiences and enhance our creativity.

- **Zooming in and out:** Changing your perspective by zooming in on details or zooming out to see the bigger picture can shift how you approach ideas, projects, or challenges.

- **Perceptual Positions:** Viewing problems from different angles or stepping into someone else's shoes provides new insights. Changing your position broadens your understanding of any situation.

- **Surprising Connections:** Innovation often comes from making unusual connections between seemingly unrelated fields. Cross-industry thinking sparks creativity.

- **The Power of Observation:** By observing the world with fresh eyes, free from preconceived notions, you unlock a wealth of creative inspiration and insight.

Journaling Prompts

- **Perception Check:** Reflect on a situation in which your initial judgment clouded your perception. What assumptions did you make? How might your experience have changed if you had approached it with fresh eyes?

- **Zoom in/Zoom out:** Think about a current project or challenge. Write about how your perspective changes when you zoom out to see the bigger picture and when you zoom in on the finer details. What new details or insights do you notice?

Exercises

- **Perception Shift Exercise:** For one week, make a conscious effort to change your perspective in everyday situations. For example, approach a conversation from the other person's point of view or observe something familiar from a new angle. At the end of the week, journal about what you learned.

- **Sensory Re-sensitization:** Choose a day to detox from overstimulation (e.g., no social media, processed food, or artificial lighting). Engage with nature, eat whole foods, and spend time in silence. Reflect on how this impacts your creativity and mood.

- **Surprising Connections Brainstorm:** Take an unrelated industry or field and try to apply one of its principles to a project or problem you're working on. Write down any innovative ideas that arise from this cross-industry thinking.

Raising the
Collective Consciousness

Only by giving are you able to receive more than you already have.
— **Jim Rohn**

As a young adult, the first time I picked up a personal development book wasn't by my own decision. My brother, who's always been passionate about the mind, universal laws, and spirituality, was the first to say, "Hey, I think you'd really benefit from this book." I believe that, for most people, this is how the journey begins. Here's why:

Personal development requires a temporary loss of status. First, we need to admit there are parts of ourselves and our lives that could use improvement. Second, we need an open mind to receive advice—often from people we don't know personally. Lastly, we must be willing to let go of our old identity to introduce a new one. Taking this step alone isn't always easy. *Would you help someone start their journey into personal development, even if it meant you wouldn't get credit for it?*

The more we support each other in raising collective consciousness, the closer we align with our best lives. Helping others on their journey also aligns with the Law of Giving: the more we give (from a genuine place), the more we receive.

Our mission at MNTALITY.com is to help every person master their mind, attention, and energy. To achieve this, we need to reach as many people as possible. Since most people do, in fact, judge a book by its cover—and its reviews—if you've found value in this book, I'd like to ask if you could leave a short review with your thoughts (which takes less than 60 seconds). Your feedback will not only help me improve future books but will also help:

... one more person manifest abundance in their life.

... one more person attract loving relationships and connections.

... one more person escape cycles of negative thinking.

... one more person reach their fullest potential.

To make this happen, scan the QR code below to leave a short review.

Thank you for your support and contribution to the collective. Now back to your scheduled programming.

Your friend,

Rynn

CHAPTER 6

Transcending Talent

◆◆◆

LAW #6:

Creativity Is a Muscle

Be regular and orderly in your life,
so that you may be violent and original in your work.
— Gustave Flaubert

Talent is overrated. Everyone has talent. Often, the only difference between people labeled as "talented" and everyone else is timing—they find their talents early. Discovering your talents at a young age depends on the era, culture, and environment you grow up in. For example, in most cultures, sports are accessible, and children with a natural inclination for athletics stand out before they turn eighteen. Another common path is music. Many children's parents expose them to instruments (such as the guitar or piano) when they're young, especially in families and cultures that value artistic expression. Early exposure to the right environments often leads to early discovery of talent.

But what about the rest of us?

When many people talk about talent, they limit it to those who excel in traditional fields, like sports or the arts. But there are countless ways to be talented. Not identifying your talent when you are young doesn't mean you don't have talent—you just haven't discovered it yet. If you feel you lack talent, believe you're destined for mediocrity, or aren't sure what your unique abilities are, this chapter is for you. We'll discuss mechanisms to uncover your natural gifts or reaffirm a skill you've known intuitively comes to you easily. Talent is not a rare trait. It's the foundation through which we can extract the most out of our creative potential. Instead of fighting your way to mediocrity, spend your life refining a natural-born ability, and become extraordinary in your domain.

Start a Project

Back in 2017, there was a massive surge of upcoming online creators—starting YouTube channels, writing books, recording podcasts, or even just posting their lifestyle on social media. The creator economy exploded and has grown exponentially—and it will only get bigger. With advancements in automation, software, and design tools, one-person businesses are becoming more common. Dreams of making a living creating art or content are more realistic today than at any other point in history.

If you want to tap into your creative potential, it's more important than ever that you have an outlet through which to express it.

Creativity is a muscle, and if you want it to get stronger, you need to train it. This means dedicating time and space to your creativity. Find your creative gym and build up your creative brawn.

In 2019, I studied environmental engineering in Madrid, Spain for six months. When I returned home from my trip, I had one thing in mind: to create a business that allowed me to live a life of freedom, creativity, and adventure. I dove into research. I invested in books, courses, and mentors. Not everything worked, but I kept the faith. I knew that if something clicked, my life would change forever.

Over the next few years, I explored a wide range of projects. I tried writing meditation manuscripts, designing audio covers, and editing soundtracks with royalty-free music. I even ran a marketing agency for chiropractors, running advertising campaigns, and learning copywriting—but the business was unsuccessful. However, with every failed attempt I was strengthening my creative muscle and honing my skills. I was doing all of this while studying engineering and working my warehouse job, packaging and shipping computer hardware.

About a year later, I discovered the path I wanted to commit to and my purpose. I would often look back and think, "Man, was I scattered and all over the place." But the truth is, I was exploring. I was diving headfirst into the unknown, immersing myself in new communities and industries. My brain was buzzing with ideas and potentials. I felt overwhelmed but I see now that this phase was crucial for my growth as a creator.

My environmental engineering degree and warehouse job weren't giving me a creative spark. I needed to find it somewhere else. The more I followed the breadcrumb trail of my excitement, the closer I was getting to my calling. When the right project aligned with my skills and vision—writing books and teaching people about my passion for metaphysics and spirituality—everything worked out.

Look for this spark. Forget about what you're going to get out of it and look for something you can obsess over. If you do something only for money, it will lack emotional connection and soul—the two key components for creating something with substance and impact. Do it for love. Indulge yourself in the creative process. With every step you take, you'll gain more clarity about your vision and hear the whispers of your calling. Once you find *the* project, pour your heart, soul, and energy into it, and don't look back.

Before discovering my major project of writing a book series, I was a dabbler—jumping from one thing to the next. And because of that, I was stuck. I got into the trap of labeling my dream as my side-project—so it never became my major project. So many people struggle to transition from working 9:00 to 5:00 to working on their purpose and passions full-time. Their side-project never takes off because it never becomes their priority physically, mentally, or energetically. The shift that needs to happen isn't always external, it's internal. It's in the meanings and definitions we give to ourselves and the activity.

The biggest part in shifting your reality is shifting your identity. Reality can only ever reflect who you are, so having a project to work on is crucial. If you want to be a creative, you need to create—and whether you're making art, music, videos, or fashion

(, or writing books), you have to actually do the work. You can't wish your way into this process. Prioritize becoming the person who's living out their dream. Stop waiting for things to work out and become someone who works them out.

Find Yourself by Creating

I've always been a deep thinker. For as long as I can remember, I've always tried to intellectualize the whys and why nots of nature and reality. I guess this is why I liked science so much. When I was a kid, I had two dream jobs in mind: to become a football player or an archeologist. The former had more to do with my upbringing and environment. The latter was a genuine interest. I wanted to spend my adult life playing in the dirt and digging out fossils. Discovering unknown terrain, uncovering Jurassic secrets, and revealing truths that had long been hidden was my genuine passion.

Before I began writing, deep thinking was something I did unconsciously and spontaneously. Spending time with friends and family, I'd find myself dissecting everyone's personality, intentions, and behaviors. Watching a movie or TV show, I'd wonder about the behind-the-scenes choices that shaped it. But before I started writing, I never had an outlet to channel these thoughts toward something meaningful or productive.

Through writing, I discovered myself. I realized just how deep a thinker I can be. Through creating content, books, emails, and now, videos, I discovered different dimensions of my truth—my preferences, tastes, and perspectives. Through creating, I could connect with the deeper layers of my soul's natural blueprint.

Most people never experience this. They wait until they know themselves before they create and share. They wait until they have the perfect clarity, the perfect skills, and the perfect story to tell. They wait until they have a diploma before they can help and inspire other people. But you don't find yourself first, then create—*you find yourself through creating*. It's through consistent expression and experimentation that you find your voice.

The most influential musicians of our time never waited until they had the perfect lyrics, instrumental licks, or unique sound to release and publish their work. Instead, they focused on getting better with every recording release. They found pieces of themselves in every failure. Through this process of self-discovery, they got closer to the right words, tone, and rhythm that resonated with them and touched everyone who listened.

Every time you create, you're getting closer to your truth.

If we were to go back and read all my old material, we'd notice how much my voice has changed. I used to sound like a timid professor on his first day of class, trying to be academic and say all the right things. The more I created, the more I let loose, and the more I let my authentic self shine.

If you're always waiting for the perfect moment to start, you're denying yourself the chance to grow, develop, and learn through the process. Artistic expression is more about self-discovery than anything else. It's not about the outcomes. It's about allowing the Universe to express and discover itself through you. The more aligned you are with this Universal desire, the more substance your creations carry. But like anything, it's a process.

Through this form of self-discovery, little by little, you shed the internal blocks and beliefs that hold you back—the layers that cover up your creative power. Authenticity takes time. However, as you peel back the layers, your inner dialogue and story shift. You open yourself up, becoming more receptive to innovative ideas and opportunities. When you open the gates to your soul, you open the gates to infinite possibility.

Be Boring

The greatest enemy of any creative endeavor is a complicated personal life. We do not have business problems. We have personal problems that reflect in our business. To maximize your creative abilities, there needs to be a certain level of simplicity and peace in your life. Too much complexity fills the brain with unnecessary information and drains your energy. When too many things are stealing your attention, there's little left for the things that matter.

David Lynch, an acclaimed filmmaker and screenwriter, is known for living a fairly predictable and "boring" life. In an interview, he said he eats the same lunch every day: tomatoes, tuna, feta cheese, and olive oil. And for dinner? You guessed it. The same thing every night: chicken and broccoli. He claimed that simplicity is a powerful tool for his creative exploration. If managed poorly, trivial things can sap you of your creative juices. By conserving the energy you might otherwise expend on things like: what you'll wear each day, what you'll eat, or what everyday chores you'll take care of, you leave more energy to be channeled elsewhere.

When your days are messy, nothing is easy. Your mind is on manual overdrive —you are trying constantly to make decisions and manage every task yourself—and you're struggling to keep up with the pull of daily life. When it's time to work on your project, you've already processed thousands of gigabytes of information and made dozens of micro-decisions. The worst-case scenario is when being messy becomes a habit, and you become someone who can't sit still and jumps from one idea to the next. Without stability, there's no foundation from which to launch your ideas. A simple way to create this foundation is through having a daily routine.

A routine outsources willpower to the subconscious mind, letting it handle mundane decisions—like when to wake up, where to go, and what chores to get done—automatically. This frees up mental energy, so you can focus on your creative pursuits.

Think of it like this. Every day you wake up with a limited reservoir of energy called your *energy budget*. Throughout the day, tasks, people, entertainment, meals, and obligations take your energy. Every time you give something your energy, you're making an investment—not just in that moment, but in your future. The key is to make a few good investments. The less you have and the better you choose, the faster you'll experience growth. Remember, where attention goes, energy flows, so funnel it efficiently.

Overcomplicating your life is self-sabotage. The more complexity that's involved, the more difficult it is to generate meaningful thoughts. We waste mental energy on trivial things, pointless drama, and empty entertainment. Simplicity opens space to channel clarity and ideas. Simplicity isn't about a lack of excitement; it's about creating a foundation from which we can explore life more meaningfully. Optimize your routine and lifestyle for simplicity. This will give you more energy to explore your creativity.

Growth Is Holistic

Reality is not black or white. It happens within a spectrum of shades of grey. There's a fine line between involving yourself passionately in a side-project during your free time and losing sleep, destroying your health, or damaging your relationships over it. As mentioned earlier, there needs to be a solid foundation from which to spring, and this foundation is supported by a few pillars—like health, relationships, finances, and happiness for example. I can't tell you what your pillars are. This is for each of us to decide on our own. Some people, might define creativity, family, or service as a pillar. Regardless of what these pillars are and how many you have, each plays a pivotal role in maintaining peace and harmony in your life. This is how you're able to grow sustainably in any domain. Without one of the pillars, everything else would come crashing down.

As creatives, often we over-exaggerate the importance of our projects and give them more meaning than we need to. This creates an imbalance between all the pillars. As a result, we also experience an imbalance in the field. The "field" refers to the energetic or mental space where our thoughts and perceptions interact with reality. It's the neutral ground from which we project meaning, shaping how we experience the world and influencing the creative process. Reality is neutral. It doesn't mean this or that. It just *is*. We are the creators of meaning, we give life meaning, and the meaning we project creates the world. Therefore, in order to experience growth, we need to harmonize the meaning that we give to the pillars and projects we have. This means reducing the importance we give to them.

Sometimes we give too much importance and meaning to things we're trying to achieve—whether it's our health, our relationships, or (especially) our projects. When we overemphasize the grandeur and magnitude of a desire, we put it on a pedestal—and keep it at an energetic distance. The solution is to pursue our goals with neutral intention. This means doing what you can, then letting go. It means acting on things you can control and accepting everything else as it comes. Try your best, then sleep easy. When you experience frustration, creative blocks, or burnout, you've likely overextended yourself.

To balance out your intentions, perceive growth as a holistic process. When you're prioritizing a project or creative endeavor, it's essential that you still give attention and care to your other pillars, whatever they may be. Without good health, you suffer. Without positive relationships, you suffer. Without happiness, you suffer. Without family, you suffer. The pillars need solid footing to bear the load. The Universe is ready to give you everything you need, but you need to be ready to receive. Otherwise, you risk losing it all.

Growth isn't always obvious. There are days when your creativity will stagnate. But that doesn't mean you should, too. Focus on improving your other pillars. Go to the gym. Spend time with family. Take yourself on a date. Relax. There are many ways to contribute indirectly to your goals. When your health is on point, you have more energy to work and be creative. When your relationships are solid, you have a support system when things go bad. When you're happy, you're more receptive to your inner genius. Every day you can be one percent better than who you were yesterday. Growth is a choice, not an outcome.

You can only do your best. Nothing else. A big part of manifestation and discovering your talent is timing. If you maintain consistency, the pillars of your life will grow even if you can't see it yet. Allow that building process to take place behind the scenes. The Universe will throw opportunities your way to level up in each pillar of your life. Accept them as they come and don't be too rigid with your priorities. Do what you can with what you have. Don't rush. What is meant for you will come.

Summary for Chapter 6: Transcending Talent
Law #6: Creativity Is a Muscle

- **Talent Is Overrated:** Talent is common; the key is discovering and refining it. Early exposure helps, but discovering your talent later in life is still possible.

- **Start a Project:** Creativity needs an outlet to grow, much like a muscle. Starting and committing to projects allows you to hone your skills and discover your calling.

- **Find Yourself Through Creation:** You don't need to wait until you "find yourself" to start creating. Self-discovery happens through the process of creating and experimenting.

- **The Importance of Routine:** A structured life helps free up mental energy, allowing for more focus on creative pursuits. Simple routines create space for inspiration to strike.

- **Simplicity over Complexity:** An overly complicated life drains energy and attention, hindering creativity. Simplifying your life helps direct energy where it matters most.

- **Holistic Growth:** Creativity is only sustainable if balanced with the other pillars of life—health, relationships, happiness, and finances.

- **Neutral Intention:** Avoid putting too much importance on any one project. Pursue your goals with dedication, but don't overburden them with meaning.

Journaling Prompts

- **Uncover Your Talent:** Reflect on your past experiences and environments. What activities brought you joy, excitement, or a sense of mastery, even if they weren't labeled as traditional talents?

- **Creative Blockers:** Think about a time when you overcomplicated a project or goal. How did this impact your creativity? What steps can you take to simplify your life now?

- **Holistic Growth:** Evaluate the pillars of your life—health, relationships, happiness, finances, and creativity. Which area feels neglected, and how can you bring more balance to it?

Exercises

- **Start a Creative Project:** Commit to a project, big or small, that excites you. Set a deadline for the first stage of completion. Track your progress and reflect on how starting this project influences your creative flow.

- **Daily Simplification:** For one week, simplify one aspect of your daily routine (e.g., your meals, wardrobe, or morning routine). Journal about how this frees up mental energy for your creative pursuits.

- **Balanced Growth Day:** Dedicate a day to nurturing all the pillars in your life—spend time with loved ones, engage in physical activity, and work on a creative project. Reflect on how each area supports your creativity and overall well-being.

CHAPTER 7

Child-Like Wonder

LAW #7:

Life Is a Game

*Man suffers only because he takes seriously
what the gods made for fun.*
— **Alan Watts**

C hildren are the ultimate creatives. Before they are conditioned to play the role of serious adults, children approach life like a game. Every moment is an opportunity to create and live out a fantasy. A game I grew up playing was cops and robbers. One team was the police force, searching and patrolling the neighborhood, while the other team, the criminals, ran and hid. In our minds, it was real, and that made the game exciting, fun, and memorable.

Memorable is the key word here. We remember things that make us feel alive—events charged with emotion stay with us, while neutral moments fade away. If we approach life with a constantly serious or neutral outlook, we'd have far fewer meaningful memories. Our art and creations are no different: if you're not emotionally invested in them, no one else will be either.

For something to have a lasting impact, it also needs to have a level of innocence and vulnerability. Think of how children draw us in. They're unafraid, and they show us how they feel and what they're thinking. One of the biggest blocks to creativity is our inability to tap into this child-like openness.

The more open we are, the more creativity flows. When we close ourselves off to our inner child, we limit our creative potential. Think about how often we do things just because it's what we "should do" or follow rules because we're "responsible adults." If you want to innovate and create something meaningful—for yourself and others—you can't just stick to the status quo.

To innovate is to create from the unknown. It's about letting yourself break the rules now and then, ignoring the scripts others might impose, and diving headfirst into curiosity, experimentation, and play. Imagine yourself as a mad scientist, questioning everything, mixing up ideas, and creating without limits. You can bring out your inner child—that part of you that always knew play is one of the purest forms of creativity.

Seriousness Is a Disease

There's an old saying that the more things change the more they stay the same: *Plus ça change, plus c'est la même chose.* The world doesn't change much. Our reality as adults operates under the same laws now as it did we were young and dumb. The only thing that changes is our perspective and where we put our attention. For example, in our western society, when you enter the workforce, have your first child, or take your first loan to purchase a home, you've entered adulthood. And what does being an adult mean? It means being responsible, behaving, and following the rules. It means acting as authority demands. It means choosing safe, secure paths. It means no more games. No more fooling around. Being professional and *taking life seriously*.

We age beyond our years not because of the passage of time, but because of how we approach life. When we approach everything with seriousness and rigidity, there is little room for creativity or fun. We narrow our perspective of the world to conform with the illusory ideas of how we should act. Of course, sometimes it's convenient and appropriate to be responsible and think about the consequences of our actions, but we should not let this stifle our creative process or minimize our worldview.

Behaving as thought everything is serious not only limits your creative potential, it hinders your mental health and well-being. Seriousness limits you based on the assumptions you make. Assumptions narrow the possibilities of every moment and create walls that block new potential from manifesting. They condense your world, keep your mind inside a small, confined box, and then, rules, expectations, and bias restrict everything you create. Nothing innovative can come from this. Within this box, more often than not, you won't find anything that resonates with the calling and impulses of your soul.

Does this mean we should just fool around like a bunch of silly middle schoolers? Of course not. But we also don't need to be so serious all the time. What we need is to have an intention. Intention operates from power and choice. When you have intention, you create boundaries and focus that guide your life in the direction you want it to go.

Intention is healthy; seriousness is like a disease. It creates tension in both the mind and body. Think about it: our bodies are capable of so many movements—we can stretch, do yoga, run, and play sports. But in our modern world, we're mostly stuck sitting or standing. Over time, that rigidity makes it harder to adapt physically—imagine trying to run a marathon after months of inactivity. The mind works the same way. We have access to endless ideas and insights, but most of us end up recycling ninety-five percent of yesterday's thoughts. When our minds become rigid, we hit blocks, and creativity struggles to flow.

The less seriously you take your work, the more innovative you become. By releasing the assumption that your work needs to be serious, you introduce a whole extra dimension of possibility. You introduce the power of play, creating fluidity and adaptability in your thinking. You also introduce the power of intention, consciously guiding your mind and reality in the direction of highest purpose and fulfillment. As I mentioned, children are creative because they assume nothing—they're open vessels. And when you become an open vessel, you can carry out greater cosmic intentions.

Breadcrumb Trail

A simple way to embody more child-like wonder is by following your excitement. For example, in the early 1990s, the renowned author of the *Harry Potter* series, J. K. Rowling, was going through a tough time. A single mother, she was unemployed and living on welfare. She'd always had a passion for writing, and according to Rowling, she was at her happiest when she was alone writing in her room. One day, on a train ride home from Manchester to her home in London, the idea of Harry Potter popped into her head. Despite her circumstances, she pursued her passion for writing and the excitement she had for this story. It took her three years to write the first book, *Harry Potter and the Sorcerer's Stone*, and many more years (and failed attempts) to get a publisher to accept it.

A simple intuitive impulse can lead you down a more fulfilling, successful, and enlightening path. However, you need to be persistent. Not every idea will be your Harry Potter, but it can lead to the next idea, which leads to the next, and so on. Follow the breadcrumb trail: with every breadcrumb you pick up, the more creative you will become and the more you will embody the frequency of a creator. The more you follow your excitement, the more the Universe will show you things to be excited about. If you live life fulfilling your excitement and passion, there is nothing else required. Everything will manifest in ways you can't even imagine.

Surrendering to your excitement opens you to deeper layers of your subconscious. For instance, while singing and dancing in the shower, an idea for an app might strike. Or, during a lighthearted family dinner, a project inspiration may spark. On vacation, you could feel a surge of creativity flow through you. These lighthearted, relaxed moments keep your mind fluid, inviting new and spontaneous connections.

Your inner child communicates with you constantly. It sees the opportunity to play and signals you through your intuition.

Throughout your day, notice your creative, intuitive impulses—and act on them. Say you're in a meeting and you crack a small joke that makes everyone laugh. That's your inner child coming out to play. Or you're listening to music, and you get the urge to dance and move to the rhythm of the song. Again, your child-like nature is coming to the fore. Or maybe, you're taking your evening walk and feel inspired to take a different route home, and you discover a beautiful garden you've never seen before. These small, seemingly insignificant moments are impulses coming from your inner child, motivating you to approach life with more curiosity and awe.

The outcome of following your intuition need not be significant at first. In fact, most of our inspiration impulses come from and lead to little things. When we act on these smaller impulses, we become more familiar with them, more trusting. Sometimes, they lead to satisfying outcomes. Sometimes, they don't. But we know one thing: they will always expand our perception of the world. The more we develop our mental comfort zone, the more room we leave for moments of inspiration.

The Universe has a reservoir of unmanifested ideas that could revolutionize the way we live in this world. When the time is right, the Universe will express these ideas through us. When we say things like "I had that same idea" or "I thought about the same thing," this is proof that the Universe has intended that an idea be expressed. The idea wasn't expressed through us because we were too distracted to notice, didn't act on it, or disregarded the idea in the name of security and predictability. One day, every innovative idea that is yet to be manifested will fall into the mind of someone who's courageous and curious enough to act on it and change the world.

In every moment, we can make a creative choice that expands and stretches our perspective and beliefs about the world. We struggle to channel infinite intelligence because we've been conditioned to follow the program ingrained in us since childhood. We can't expect our lives to change or expect anything we create to have any impact if it's coming from the same level of mind each time.

Following your excitement and passion is not only an act of creativity—it's an act of exploration. It widens your scope of what's possible. Genius ideas come from novel combinations that can happen only if you step into the unknown. When you have more elements to work with, there are more possible combinations. When you have a larger collection of experiences and ideas, your creative potential expands and you discover new elements that can further your creative process in the present or future. By following your excitement, you elevate your creativity.

Ideas Are Everywhere

Child-like wonder and curiosity have the power to turn nothing into something. When I was a kid, we didn't need a lot to have fun. For example, a box wasn't just a container for storing stuff. It was a car we could slide down the stairs. It was a tank to go into battle with friends and siblings. It was a fort to protect our territory. It was a house to live, eat, and sleep in. It was a cave to explore the dark and tell spooky stories. A box was more than just a box. Simplicity birthed our creative ideas.

Ideas are everywhere. They can arise from both internal and external reflection. Pondering an idea or meditating in silence can produce the same level of inspiration as observing nature. Just as watching birds fly can spark an idea, meditation can help you connect with a deeper truth. There is no lack of ideas or inspiration in the world—they are inside us and all around us. What we lack is a keen perception of what's right in front of us. We create our experiences through our perception. Similarly, ideas aren't created, they are perceived.

Two people can look at a tree and have two different experiences. One person might get bored and want to leave, while another might marvel at how its roots keep the tree in place despite strong winds. Or how its leaves are growing toward the sun, following the laws of phototropism. There are infinite lessons we can learn and ideas we can source from every experience. Most of us just choose to ignore them.

Every moment has something to teach you. Here's another Japanese philosophy: Ichigo-ichie (一期一会). This translates roughly to "one time, one moment." This is the concept of appreciating the unrepeatable nature of every moment. No two experiences are ever the same. Never again in the history of the cosmos will anyone experience this moment (as I'm writing this and you're reading this). If you observe a tree today, you won't have the same experience when you see it tomorrow. The tree might look the same, but there will be nuances: how you're feeling, the time of day, the angle of the sun, the strength of the wind.

When you can embrace this philosophy in your own life, something that might seem ordinary or regular to an average person can be a source of inspiration for you to create a work of literature, a piece of music, or a business product.

Everything has the potential to be a source of inspiration. When you open up to this, you embody the way of the artist. You can combine elements that nobody has ever mixed before and create something nobody has ever created. The Universe is filled with ideas and inspiration. Child-like wonder is about embracing the world as your playground and believing that life is a game. Everything around you can be used, reinterpreted, broken down, or magnified to create a something that resonates with your unique vision. For someone who taps into their inner child, there are no limits.

Summary for Chapter 7: Child-Like Wonder
Law #7: Life Is a Game

- **Children Are Creative by Nature:** Children approach life as a game, engaging in pure creativity with innocence and openness. This unconditioned way of thinking can unlock vast creative potential.

- **Memorable Experiences Have Emotion:** For art and creations to have a lasting impact, they must evoke emotion. Emotional investment brings creativity to life.

- **Seriousness Limits Creativity:** Taking life too seriously stifles creativity. A playful, curious attitude opens the mind to new possibilities.

- **Follow Your Excitement:** Excitement and passion lead to greater creativity. Following the "breadcrumb trail" of excitement fosters innovation and opens doors to new ideas.

- **Ideas Are Everywhere:** Creativity is not about creating new things from scratch but perceiving the world differently. Everything around us is a source of inspiration.

- **Big Potential in Little Things:** Like a child turning a simple box into endless imaginary scenarios, expand your awareness to see possibilities in seemingly insignificant things.

Journaling Prompts

- **Remember Your Childhood Joys:** What games or activities did you love as a child? How did those experiences spark creativity or a sense of wonder? How can you bring some of that playful energy into your life now?

- **Breaking Seriousness:** Reflect on areas in your life where you may be taking things too seriously. How is this limiting your creativity? What small steps can you take to introduce more playfulness into those areas?

- **Breadcrumb Trail of Excitement:** What excites you today? Write about an idea or project that sparks excitement, even if it seems small or insignificant. How can you nurture this excitement into a creative pursuit?

Exercises

- **Play Day:** Set aside a day or a few hours to "play" with no specific agenda. Engage in activities that bring you joy—whether it's drawing, dancing, or exploring nature—and notice how your creativity flows when you're not focused on outcomes.

- **Idea Generation Walk:** Go for a walk and observe your surroundings with fresh eyes. Notice details you usually overlook. When you return, write down any thoughts or ideas that come to mind, no matter how small. This practice helps you tap into the infinite ideas the world offers.

- **Reinterpret an Object:** Take a simple object in your home, like a cup, a pencil, or a box. Brainstorm five new uses for it, just as you would have as a child. This exercise encourages thinking beyond conventional uses and seeing things from a new perspective.

CHAPTER 8

Inspiration Is Waiting

◆◆◆

LAW #8:

Luck Is Preparation

Inspiration exists, but it has to find you working.
— **Pablo Picasso**

In 1665, the great plague once again spread across Europe. Fearing getting infected, thousands of civilians moved or isolated themselves. During this time, Sir Isaac Newton, an English physicist and mathematician at the University of Cambridge, returned to his family home in Woolsthorpe, Lincolnshire, as everything was forced to close.

According to legend, one evening, while sitting in his garden under an apple tree, an apple struck his head. This sparked his thinking: why the apple had fallen, and what forces caused it to fall? He pondered the event and wondered how this potential force might be responsible for not just the apple falling, but for keeping the moon in orbit around the Earth, and the planets in orbit around the sun. This singular moment led to one of the most revolutionary theories in the world of science: the theory of gravity.

When we think of inspiration, we think of stories like Sir Isaac Newton's. A moment of godly brilliance and timing that comes like a strike of lightning. One place, one time. Rare. Spontaneous. Random. We think of inspiration as a treasure that happens only for those lucky enough to stumble upon it. But it's not true. Inspiration knocks on the door of our mental faculties all day long. There is a shower of insights, ideas, and epiphanies ready to drop into our inner dialogue. The problem? Most people aren't receptive to them. The conversations we're having internally and externally aren't compatible with the reality we're seeking. We're distracted. Scattered. Focused on things that drain our attention and energy.

It's like we're watching the news on max volume, so we don't hear the doorbell ring. The Universe is trying to deliver the goods, but we're ignoring it—most of the time, unconsciously.

Inspiration isn't about luck. It's about preparation. It's about lowering the volume and preparing yourself to receive. The more receptive you become, the more often inspiration strikes. It's like setting up a lightning pole inside your mind. When you commit to a project, the pole will attract ideas from every corner of your environment and subconscious. Many won't be good—in fact, most won't be. Your mind must be open for the good idea to enter. And when the right idea comes, it's like striking gold.

The Gatekeeper

The subconscious mind can store a vast amount of data—far more than we can consciously process at any given time. With every moment that passes, it continuously absorbs information about our physical environment, thoughts, and emotions. To manage this overwhelming influx, the mind creates a filter that separates what's relevant from what's irrelevant, based on our current circumstances and the identity our ego seeks to maintain. As a result, we only pay attention to what we consider important in the moment.

Our subconscious mind is our most powerful tool for creativity. Tapping into its hidden reservoir unlocks a potent source of inspiration—nothing else comes close. Within it lies information we've seen, read, or heard, any of which could change the trajectory of our lives. However, a gatekeeper—the ego—often prevents us from accessing this vast potential.

As noted earlier, the beliefs you carry are shaped through conditioning, and over time, they become habits and patterns. These form the constructs of your ego, which uses them to protect you from what it perceives as harm. However, the ego is really protecting itself, keeping you confined to the limited space it's created. The subconscious mind holds information that could motivate you to step beyond who you've been, which threatens the ego's control.

Popular figures like Salvador Dalí and Thomas Edison bypassed the gatekeeper with a technique known as *hypnagogic napping*. Both Dalí and Edison would sit in a chair holding a small object—Edison used a ball, and Dalí a metal key—between their fingers.

Underneath, they placed a metal plate that would make noise if something were to hit it. As they drifted into the hypnagogic state (the drowsy state between wakefulness and sleep), their mind and muscles would relax, causing the object to slip from their hand, fall, and strike the plate. The sound would immediately wake them, allowing them to recall and capture any fleeting ideas or images from this creative, semi-dreamlike state. They relaxed so much; it allowed them to bypass the gatekeeper and access a reservoir of creativity.

For most of us, the subconscious mind is accumulating dust. It holds on to quality information we've absorbed from books, courses, podcasts, and videos, but we rarely access it, let alone apply it. This leads to analysis paralysis. You want to learn and grow, but your gatekeeper is stopping you from using this information to promote change and growth. Fears and doubts limit your mental faculties and block the flow of inspiration.

The solution? *Develop receptivity.* Open your subconscious mind to access different layers of your being. Think differently. If you keep thinking the same thoughts in the same way all the time, nothing innovative will emerge. Just like a tense muscle, you need to stretch your mind. However, becoming more receptive requires you to first understand the mental patterns that are keeping you stuck.

Many cognitive biases block people from accessing new information and ideas. These include patterns like expertise bias, the sunk cost fallacy, groupthink, cognitive dissonance, and functional fixedness. Let's look at each one:

◊ Expertise Bias

Sometimes, experts are not willing to explore new information. They think they know. And because of this, there's no room to grow and learn. They limit themselves to a box of knowledge and information, blocking out the possibility of receiving inspiration and creating innovation. When you approach a project with the mind of an expert, check that you're not operating from only what you know. Make sure you are operating from a place of soul instead of ego, and that you are becoming a vessel for the Universe rather than a vessel for your beliefs.

◊ The Sunk Cost Fallacy

After spending years investing in one career path or project, it's unlikely someone would want to switch away from it. They fear starting over. They fear going back to zero. But most importantly, they fear admitting they've sacrificed so much for something that isn't what they thought it would be. This is the sunk cost fallacy, and it keeps many of us stuck on an unfulfilling path—one that doesn't spark our creativity and lacks a substantial return. Understand that the sooner you catch this and shift your focus, the sooner you'll manifest the life you desire.

◊ Groupthink

In a group setting, the desire to maintain peace and harmony often stops individuals from thinking outside the box. They suppress their opinions and creative ideas in the name of comfort. This lack of diversity in thought can hold back the group from considering alternative paths, ultimately stifling innovation. To avoid this, encourage open dialogue and create an environment where all ideas are welcomed—especially the unconventional ones. Remember, innovation thrives when everyone feels safe to contribute without fear of judgment.

◊ Cognitive Dissonance

When we first get into personal development, we're often motivated to review and audit our belief systems. This is helpful in pinpointing and dissolving the internal blocks that hold us back from stepping into the highest version of ourselves. Here's where it gets tricky: we only question the beliefs we're open to letting go of. We don't question the ones we truly hold on to. When we encounter new information or evidence that challenges our deeply held beliefs, we're quick to reject it or defend our position with rational arguments. We try to avoid discomfort (or cognitive dissonance).

To grow, we must get comfortable with discomfort. Instead of defending your beliefs, practice sitting with that discomfort and asking yourself why you feel so strongly about them. This will open the door for deeper insight and transformation.

◊ Functional Fixedness

Our education system was created for the industrial revolution. It teaches us to become linear thinkers. One plus one equals two. Through this line of thinking, every object, tool, or idea is approached traditionally. We use and apply them as they have always been used and applied. What many people don't realize (or aren't open to) is that there are many ways to approach a problem or use a tool. For instance, a paperclip holds papers together, but it can also pick a lock, reset a device, or be used as a hook from which to hang things. An object or idea isn't what limits us—it's our perception of it.

To break free from linear thinking, challenge yourself to look at everyday tools, concepts, or situations from different angles. Ask yourself, "What else can this be used for?" or "How can this approach be applied in a new way?" Innovation starts when you shift how you perceive what's in front of you.

You can have all the knowledge, skills, and good intentions, but if you can't get past the gatekeeper, you're just treading water, replicating the past. You'll never move forward, and you'll stagnate—the opposite of being creative. A closed mind, limited to facts, rules, and knowns, is not receptive to inspiration. To truly embody creativity, you need an open mind. This means being willing to explore, experiment, and be proven wrong.

The Beginner's Mind

In Buddhism, the term *shoshin* (初心) translates to Beginner's Mind. This philosophy is about having an attitude of openness and receptivity. A Beginner's Mind reflects an open mind—one that is empty and receptive to new ideas and inspiration. If you want to touch reality and expand your world, you must empty yourself of the deeply ingrained intellectual patterns and tendencies generated by the ego.

A Beginner's Mind requires the act of letting go. When you let go of preconceived notions, you come closer to reality. This is an essential step in the process of enlightenment. Emptying the mind can also dissolve personal or egoic ambitions that cloud how we approach life. A Beginner's Mind is receptive to divine timing, allowing you to become a vortex that attracts the right information, ideas, and insights at the right moments.

Often, when we approach a problem or idea, we cloud it with assumptions that narrow our perception. A narrowed perception creates a narrowed reality. The mind can impede divine intervention. The answer to a problem we face might be obvious, but because our thinking is cluttered with rigid thoughts and beliefs, we cannot recognize it. We often say, "Why didn't I think of that?" This happens because we can't see beyond the scope of our conditioning. The concept of Beginner's Mind teaches us to think beyond our biases and to consider information that challenges traditional ways of approaching a situation.

In my coaching program, I introduce clients to a process known as No-Box Thinking. As creatives, we often limit ourselves to sourcing information either from inside the box of knowns or outside the box, in the unknown. But what if there were no box at all? What if the idea of a "box" was merely an illusion we create in our minds? Reality is interconnected in countless ways. When we frame a problem in relation to a box, we segregate our thoughts and ideas. No-Box Thinking is about approaching a problem directly from its source, rather than from the labels and names we place on it.

Over time, we develop intellectual overconfidence in subjects we're familiar with or have studied extensively. This conditioning of expertise doesn't just happen in the mind; it also happens in our emotions. Feeling like an expert can lead to a closed mind. Beginner's Mind isn't just about thinking like a beginner—it's about feeling like one.

When we let go of emotions associated with pride and personal ambition, we become more sensitive to our intuition. Instead of trying to impose our expertise on the Universe, we allow the Universe to be the expert, guiding us down alternative paths. Embracing Beginner's Mind puts us in a position to receive guidance that leads us to our highest service, contribution, and fulfillment.

The mind is loud. We naturally close ourselves off to new information because we're already trying to process so much. A mind filled to the brim with judgments, negativity, and narratives is too heavy and cluttered to receive anything new. Approaching life with an open mind helps us dissolve these thoughts, as we realize there is more to life than meets the eye. We can ask questions like, "What if there's another way? What if this isn't true? What if I'm wrong?" The more we question our thoughts, the more space we open up.

New information doesn't always lead to innovation. We already consume a lot of information daily—that's not the problem. The problem is that we close ourselves off to possibility. We need to become receptive to possibility. For the beginner, there are infinite paths to achieve a goal. For the expert, there are few. The more paths you notice or consider, the more opportunities you'll have, and the more insights you'll gain.

Prepare for the Wave

When I was in Costa Rica back in 2022, I did a thirty-day surfing challenge. Every day, I woke up at 6:00 a.m. and hit the water. After each session, I walked home and watched every type of surfing tutorial video you can imagine—from how to position yourself on the board to the best type of fin to use.

For the first few days, my biggest struggle was catching a wave. Rarely did I stand up. In any one-hour session, I had one to three chances to stand up and catch a wave—often leading to wipeouts. I was either too far along the shoulder of the wave, paddling hard but not having enough power to drop into it, or I was too close to the peak, and the wave crashed over me.

After a little research, I figured out that positioning yourself to catch the wave is one of the most efficient ways of surfing, because the wave will do the work for you. The "sweet spot" is slightly next to the peak. To find it, I'd spend a few minutes on the beach scanning the ocean, noting where the waves were breaking and pinpointing the sweet spot from the sand before entering the water.

There's a lot more nuance to this, but surfing taught me a valuable lesson. If you want to catch a wave of inspiration and ideas, you need to put yourself in the metaphorical sweet spot—where it takes less effort to come up with innovative, creative thoughts. Like waves in the ocean, waves of inspiration are passing through us constantly. We don't catch them because we're not in the water. We're not playing the game, doing the work, and *creating*. Inspiration doesn't come to those who wait for it, it comes to those that jumped into the ocean of possibility. To wait is to expect to get something from nothing. The Universe rewards intention. For every action, there is a reaction—no action, no reaction.

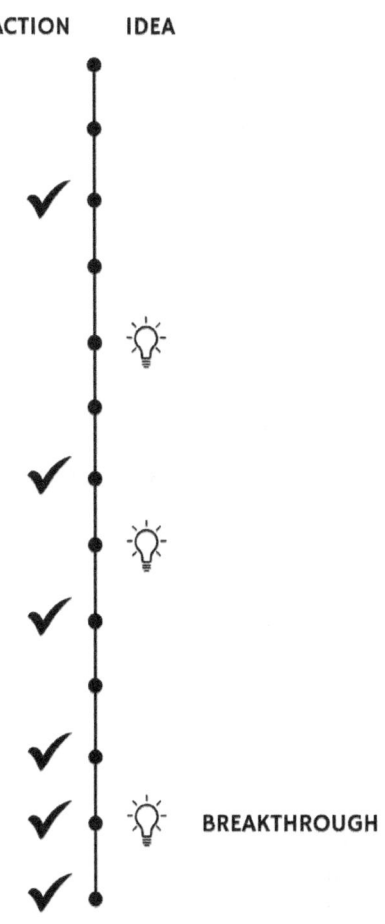

We can't control the timing of the tides. We can't control the timing of life. Before getting in the water, reflect on where your sweet spot is. Think about places you can go, people you can speak to, or content you can consume that will inspire you. Epiphanies can't be timed or predicted, but you can increase the probability of them happening. The waves roll in and change when we least expect them. They're fast or slow. Big or small. We never know. To catch the best wave, position yourself to catch it. Be ready to receive ideas when they come.

As noted earlier, the subconscious mind accumulates information every day. When the information it accumulates has nothing to do with what you're trying to create or achieve, it'll never output anything productive. Every thought you generate will distract you from the project you want to nurture. The key is to fill your mind with better information. For your mind to nurture you, nurture it.

Give your mind direction with action. By taking action, you're programming yourself to find creative solutions and ideas. By sitting down and taking time to do the work, you're giving your subconscious mind information to work with. When the day ends, your subconscious is still working in the background, generating ideas. The next time you sit down to create, you'll be filled with new insights.

If you find yourself stuck in the creative process, start small. Set a daily minimum goal so achievable it's impossible to procrastinate. Often, you'll find yourself exceeding that goal. For example, I had a client who was procrastinating on her book. We set a daily target of just 200 words. This simple, low-pressure commitment took the weight off the task, and she often wrote far more than planned—ultimately finishing her book in record time. The biggest hurdle for creatives is simply starting. Turning the key to the engine is all it takes to get moving. Most of us never turn that key, and that's why we remain stuck.

When I first started writing books, I had read nearly a hundred books. My subconscious mind knew what a good book looked like, sounded like, and felt like. So, when I started writing my own, I knew what direction I wanted to go in. Immerse yourself in the world of your craft. If you're an engineer, reading books on surfing might be fun to explore beyond your niche or industry, but it's books on engineering that are going to put your subconscious to work and connect the right dots.

Similarly, you can't find information about Italian cuisine in a Thai cookbook. You can spend all day reading, hoping you'll find the recipe for spaghetti Bolognese in its pages—but you never will. You need to change your source material. If you want to create the best recipe, fill your mind with the best ingredients. For example, if you want to write a novel, immerse yourself in the work of people you admire or who have succeeded before you. Study character development, plot structure, and writing styles. Give yourself quality information from which to source inspiration. If you're starting a business, surround yourself with other business owners in your industry. Consume content, take courses, and read books that reflect the goals you're trying to achieve.

Preparation is the simplest way to approach creativity. You've heard everything I'm saying before—it's nothing new. However, I'm saying it to remind you that luck comes to those who are prepared to receive it. You can't think your way to inspiration. You need to move toward it. It's waiting for you.

Summary for Chapter 8: Inspiration Is Waiting
Law #8: Luck Is Preparation

- **Inspiration Is Everywhere:** Inspiration isn't random; it's constantly available, but most people aren't receptive to it because of distractions and mental clutter.

- **Preparation Unlocks Inspiration:** Being mentally prepared and engaged in your craft allows inspiration to flow naturally. It's not about luck but about creating the right conditions to receive ideas.

- **Overcoming Mental Blocks:** Biases like expertise bias, sunk cost fallacy, and groupthink often prevent new ideas from being considered. Recognizing and dissolving these biases opens the door to inspiration.

- **Develop a Beginner's Mind:** Maintaining an open, curious mindset (Beginner's Mind) allows you to see fresh possibilities and solutions, free from rigid expectations.

- **No-Box Thinking:** Let go of limiting beliefs and approaches. Instead of thinking inside or outside the box, eliminate the box entirely to approach challenges from a more expansive perspective.

- **Position Yourself for Ideas:** Like a surfer looking for the sweet spot to catch a wave, you need to position yourself in environments and communities where inspiration can strike.

- **Consistent Action Attracts Ideas:** Taking regular action on your projects sets up your subconscious mind to generate creative insights, even when you're not actively working on them.

Journaling Prompts

- **Recognizing Mental Blocks:** Reflect on areas in your life where you might be limiting your creativity because of biases like expertise bias, groupthink, or the sunk cost fallacy. How can you challenge these biases to create space for new ideas?

- **Developing Beginner's Mind:** Think about a project or area of your life where you've been approaching things with a closed mind. What would happen if you let go of your assumptions and approached it with curiosity and openness?

- **Positioning for Inspiration:** What actions can you take today to position yourself in the "sweet spot" for inspiration? Consider the environments, people, and content that could fuel your creativity.

Exercises

- **Inspiration Inventory:** Take a week to actively fill your mind with content, ideas, and experiences related to your creative goals (e.g., reading books, listening to podcasts, or visiting new places). At the end of the week, write down any new insights or ideas that have surfaced.

- **Beginner's Day:** Spend a day doing something entirely new, whether it's learning a new skill or exploring a new environment. As you go through the day, notice how having a Beginner's Mind makes you more open to inspiration.

- **Hypnagogic napping:** Practice capturing ideas like Salvador Dalí and Thomas Edison. Loosely hold an object over a hard surface and try to fall asleep. When the sound of the object falling wakes you up, jot down any ideas that surfaced.

CHAPTER 9

Multi-Dimensional Thinking

---◆◆---

LAW #9:

All Solutions Are Creative Solutions

The real voyage of discovery consists not in seeking new landscapes,
but in having new eyes.
— **Marcel Proust**

I n my high school biology class, our teacher, Mr. Lima, held up a glass of water with a few cubes of ice. He asked the class, "Can anybody tell me what's happening here?" Students raised their hands. "The ice is cooling down the water," "The temperature of the water is dropping," and "The cup is filling up," were a few of the answers. He shook his head. "Those are not the answers I'm looking for. When people put ice in water, they expect it to cool down the water, but this is not what's happening. The truth is, the water is melting the ice. And through this process, the water gets cooler."

Aside from enlightening moments like these, the education system has limited our perception of reality. Reality has more to offer than we can see with our two eyes. Reality is multi-dimensional, but we've been trained to perceive from a two-dimensional lens. School didn't teach us to think. It gave us information from which to source our thoughts. It gave us textbooks with facts we had to remember.

Think of it this way: your mind starts out like a majestic cathedral—full of colors, shapes, imagery, and intricate architecture. But once we enter the school system, this cathedral gets reconstructed into a plain, grey building with one long hallway. Each door down that hall leads to a different room labeled with a subject: "business," "politics," "mathematics," "music," and so on. Inside each room, boxes are neatly stacked with files that range from beginner to expert levels.

Later in life, when we face a problem, we instinctively head to the relevant room, open the right box, and pull out what we know. But here's the catch: we don't mix subjects. If you're solving a business problem, you stick to the business room. If you need medical advice, you go to the medicine room. The more education we acquire, the more rooms and boxes we accumulate. However, when thinking is confined to these labeled boxes, imagination takes a back seat, and problem-solving becomes limited to what's memorized. No wonder they say, "The more you know, the less you see."

This segregation of thoughts has limited our ability to see the interconnected parts of our reality. We struggle to see the positive in the negative, the light in the dark, and to find unique solutions to unique problems. It prevents us from blending dissimilar subjects to create a unique combination that changes the world. Examples are all around us: the smartphone (phone + computer), Airbnb (online listing + bed & breakfast), the typewriter (piano + writing), and the electric toothbrush (toothbrush + electric motor). Creative thinking is generating novel combinations to discover a new concept or approach.

If you can't think creatively, you're holding back the true power of your mind—and you'll spend your life recycling the same thoughts. Each idea will echo the one before it. Every problem you try to solve will be drawn from the same box of familiar solutions. Your experiences, too, will start to blend into one another, making life feel like a loop of sameness. Contrary to popular belief, linear thinking isn't the answer to every problem. It might check off a few practical needs, but when you're hungry for a breakthrough, all you'll find are the same old ideas, rehashed.

The path to expanding your reality is creativity. Creative thinking is about widening your perception of a situation or problem so your broader perspective introduces new possibilities. This becomes even more relevant when you're facing a challenge or obstacles you've never faced before.

Everyone has unique problems, and no two problems are ever the same. On the surface, problems might look similar, but they're not. A wider context differentiates one problem from the other, so there is not a one-size-fits-all solution to anything. We can get pretty close to finding a solution that works for many people, but it doesn't work for everyone, because everyone has a different upbringing, background, and biology. Therefore, the solution to your problems will not always come from regular, everyday thinking. We've been taught to see things the same way everyone else sees them and to approach problems, seek solutions, and find answers the same way it's always been done.

If you approach life in the same way everyone has always approached it, you'll never find answers to problems no one has ever solved. It's crucial for you to learn the skill of multi-dimensional thinking.

The Essence

When we look at a problem or when we're trying to come up with an idea, often, superficial elements like labels, categories, or niches that define our subject distract us. For example, if you were building a car, you'd look into past car projects and study how cars are made, then reproduce the same system. This is how the average person thinks. They stick to the status-quo. They pick up a textbook. But what about geniuses? How do they think?

We go to school, and we're taught about Albert Einstein's discoveries and theories about the Universe, but never are we taught how he learned to think, what his habits were, how he looked at the world, how he spoke, how he interacted with other people, or how he determined what was worth and not worth observing or studying. Einstein's discoveries didn't happen coincidentally—they arose from thinking processes and intentions that went against the traditional views of science and society. Albert Einstein wasn't a logical thinker; he was a creative one.

Going back to our car example, when Henry Ford made the intention to create the Model T, he couldn't get any insight from those who came before him because what he created was the first of its kind. Instead of looking at how cars are made, he looked into "how things are made" and "how things are taken apart." He looked into the essence of the problem he was trying to solve.

One day, he visited a slaughterhouse. The process of butchering livestock was outside his wheelhouse and outside of logical reasoning, but his visit inspired the idea of the assembly line that made creating the Model T possible. By combining two novel concepts, he revolutionized the automobile industry.

In creative thinking, start with "the essence." Look into the principle of why things work. When you can zoom in to the function and ignore the labels, you're being flexible. This is how you find tools and tactics that serve the idea you want to bring to fruition. Otherwise, you'll just distract and limit yourself with approaches that fail to work.

When you focus on the function, as opposed to the label, you widen the mental scope of what's possible. Then you can expand your search into other fields that have already found a solution to the problem you want to solve.

When I published my first book, I knew that if I wanted it to be successful, I needed to differentiate myself. I was jumping into a niche that had hundreds of established authors and hundreds of new authors self-publishing every day. I wanted to come up with a good title and blurb for the book. My fellow authors kept their titles and descriptions simple. Some had published their books years (sometimes decades) ago and had leveraged the marketing of the publishing house and the brand they had built. I was twenty-three and had no brand or publishing house to leverage. So, instead of copying what had already been done, I looked at the essence of "what makes things go viral" and "what makes a book a good book." By attracting people's attention with a good hook and providing immense value inside the book, I increased the probability of it working out. I explored and my search led me to YouTube.

YouTube can make regular people sub-celebrities overnight. All it takes is the right hook, thumbnail, and content in a video. When searching the topic "manifesting," I found videos that had gone viral using words like "technique" paired with persuasive words and phrases. This is where I got the idea for the subtitle of my first book, *15 Techniques to Attract Your Best Life, Even if You Think It's Impossible Now*. Within a year, it was ranked above the books of people I used to study and look up to.

When you look for the essence of something, novel combinations of ideas and concepts are easier to come by. Without understanding a thing's essence, it's a lot harder to come by an idea that makes sense or is valid. When you understand the "why," the "what" is easier to find.

Steal Like an Artist

Everything comes from something. The evolution of nature happens in stacks. One combination, mixture, or interaction at a time—two subjects that already exist coming together to create a third subject. This is how nature evolves. Just as nature doesn't skip steps in the process of evolution, we can't skip steps in the creative process. A work of art that manifests into the world results from material already present—so we already have everything we need to be creative. We just need to put the puzzle pieces together.

As we have seen, creative ideas come from a combination of things that already exist. When you see a painting, read a book, or purchase a product, they are always the manifestation of someone who looked at an existing element and mixed it with other elements.

If you try to create something from nothing, you'll almost always find yourself stuck. You'll play a waiting game, hoping, wishing, and begging for the right idea to pop into your mind. But you create by creating. You create by stacking and connecting pieces together. Sometimes they work. Sometimes they don't. Often, we never know why they do or don't. But we can get pretty close.

One way to apply the practice of stealing like an artist is by studying the greats in your field. By compiling references from which to source your ideas, you can study material, art, or businesses that have experienced success in the past. In copywriting and marketing, this is known as your *swipe file*—a collection of successful headlines, hooks, descriptions, and advertisements that you can use as inspiration to create your own. From here, you grab elements you like and disregard what you don't like. True creativity requires clarity—what resonates with your soul? What doesn't?

Once you have clarity, the next step is to, again, look at the essence. Why do you like this or that? Why do you dislike this or that? What about the subject or material attracts or repels you? What is the function of the things you like? Knowing your preferences gives you direction on how to express yourself authentically.

Pablo Picasso studied a variety of art styles, everything from realism to African to ancient Iberian sculptures. Classical techniques felt limiting, so he explored other areas that could spark his inspiration and expand his perception of art. By adopting different perspectives, he curated a style he liked. Eventually, in collaboration with French artist Georges Braque, he developed his own style known as Cubism—manifested by combining elements from multiple different sources of inspiration. This distinct artwork is displayed in museums and galleries around the world. The moral of this story is: don't think about creating without first thinking about combining!

Introduce Randomness

Often, genius strikes in unexpected ways: like Isaac Newton discovering gravity from a falling apple, Henry Ford developing the assembly line from visiting a slaughterhouse, and de Mestral inventing Velcro after a walk in the Alps. Randomness has always been a part of the creative process. However, in a world that pushes the idea of habits, structure, and routine, often, we do not recognize the role spontaneity and randomness have in the creative process.

Not only does introducing an element of randomness to your creative endeavors train you to apply the concepts we've covered in this chapter, it adds an air of uniqueness to your work. By connecting seemingly unrelated subjects, you discover there's more to them than meets the eye.

When you put two subjects side-by-side, like a toothbrush and an electric motor, your mind thinks of ways of making these two pieces fit together. A brush that cleans motors? Not efficient. An electric motor that powers a toothbrush? Genius. By training yourself to see the link between all things, you could revolutionize your art or your industry.

Brian Eno, a world-renowned music producer, created a deck of cards known as *Oblique Strategies*. These cards inspire musicians and artists to come up with new ideas by drawing a card with a random question, challenge, or element and introducing them to their work. This process fuels creative juices and helps users overcome creative blocks. A card might suggest a challenge like "recreate an old idea," "abandon normal instruments" or "try faking it!" The questions are vague enough to allow the user to come up with their own answers and direction. This simple practice influenced countless artists, including big names like U2 and David Bowie. Give the Universe a chance to provide you with a source of inspiration you could never see coming.

In his book, *A Treatise of Painting*, Leonardo da Vinci wrote you could find ideas by simply observing stains on a wall. He mentioned how Botticelli used to get inspiration for his landscape art by throwing a sponge soaked in paint at a blank wall and contemplating the randomness of the confused mass of ink. The irregular shapes, colors, and formations would stretch his brain and force him to find something where most people would find nothing. One way we practice this is when we look at the clouds, and see animals, objects, people, and scenes with nothing but our imagination. "Although it seems of little import and good for a laugh," da Vinci wrote, "it is nonetheless of great utility in bringing out the creativity in some of these inventions." Introducing randomness allows us the opportunity to share with the world a perspective nobody has ever had before, pushing us slightly beyond the edge of what's possible.

Radical approaches push the boundaries of what's deemed acceptable. Most people operate from only one portion of the spectrum. From only one room in the hallway. Test how far you can push your creativity by exploring the extremes and peeking over to see "the other side." Calling an outdated piece of clothing "vintage" gives a modern twist to a garment previously considered worn out. Graffiti, once seen as vandalism, has evolved into a respected, sophisticated art form. Reclaimed wood, once discarded as scrap, is now used and sold as high-end rustic furniture. Explore the opposite side of the spectrum, and you might notice something most people haven't.

Let everything life throws at you inspire you. Your only limits are in your imagination. Remember we talked earlier about the concept that all is One? We're all connected. Everything you see, hear, smell, taste, or touch can inspire your ability to bring forth an innovative idea the world has yet to see.

Summary for Chapter 9: Multi-Dimensional Thinking
Law #9: All Solutions Are Creative Solutions

- **Breaking Away from Traditional Thinking:** We're taught to be linear thinkers. However, true creativity arises when we break free from these traditional constraints and approach problems from multiple dimensions.

- **Seek the Essence of Problems:** Instead of focusing on surface-level categories and labels, look for the essence of a problem. This allows you to make connections between seemingly unrelated concepts.

- **Creativity Through Combination:** Creativity results from combining existing elements in new ways. Instead of waiting for inspiration, actively seek and combine ideas, objects, and experiences to create something novel.

- **Introducing Randomness for Innovation:** Spontaneity can spark breakthroughs. By introducing random elements or ideas into your creative process, you can push the boundaries of ordinary thinking and find unique, unexpected solutions.

- **Thinking Like an Artist:** Stealing like an artist means borrowing and combining elements from multiple sources to create something new. Study the work of others, but always focus on how it resonates with you and aligns with your authentic vision.

- **Expanding Perception:** Multi-dimensional thinking is about expanding your perception to see beyond the obvious. Blend ideas, be random, and explore the other side of the spectrum.

Journaling Prompts

- **Essence of Problems:** Think about a current problem or project you're working on. Instead of focusing on the surface details, ask yourself, "What is the essence of this problem?" "How can you I apply principles from different fields to solve it creatively?"

- **Random Inspiration:** Reflect on a time when an unexpected source of inspiration helped you solve a problem. How can you intentionally introduce randomness into your current projects intentionally to spark fresh ideas?

- **Steal Like an Artist:** Choose three of your favorite creative works (books, songs, or pieces of art). What specific elements from each do you resonate with, and how can you combine them to influence your own work?

Exercises

- **The Essence Challenge:** Pick an object or concept you're familiar with and break it down to its essence. Ask yourself, "What is this really about?" Then think of unrelated fields that solve similar problems, and brainstorm ways to apply their solutions to your situation.

- **Build Your Swipe File:** Create a swipe file of creative works you admire, including titles, designs, concepts, and more. Analyze why they stand out to you, then use elements of them as inspiration for your own projects.

CHAPTER 10

Forged by Fire

LAW #10:

There Is Purpose in Struggle

Out of suffering have emerged the strongest souls;
the most massive characters are seared with scars.
— **Kahlil Gibran**

I've met a lot of entrepreneurs and creatives over the years who thrive in their field. They push the boundaries of what's possible and exceed expectations, earning their dreamed-of income and making an impact in the world. Behind each one is a hero's story with challenges and struggles. It's difficult to find someone who's following their highest path successfully without having slayed a few demons along the way.

There's purpose in suffering. Every battle you face opens you up and brings you closer to who you are. Your trials and tribulations leave scars that remind you of why you started your journey in the first place, but they also become a source of inspiration. Many of the greatest creations in history came from people, experiences, and sources forged in fire. The strongest steel always comes from the hottest coals.

Your Painful Advantage

We often pick up personal development books (like this one) to avoid struggle. But if you expose yourself to the outside world, it's difficult to avoid conflict altogether. If you're in pursuit of a greater goal, inevitably, challenges and obstacles will play a part in your journey. It's virtually impossible to become a greater version of yourself without first overcoming situations that push you to expand and grow. This is the nature of evolution.

When an eagle chick is ready to hatch, it must break out of its shell using its beak and muscles. This physically demanding process is known as pipping. It strengthens the chick, so when it hatches, it can thrive and adapt to life outside the egg. If someone were to intervene in this process, the weak, underdeveloped chick would have difficulty surviving. Struggle gives you the strength to create and live a purpose-driven existence, and simultaneously, to serve as a source of inspiration for yourself and others.

A good story has six elements: the introduction, inciting incident, rising action, climax, falling action, and conclusion. The first three describe the beginning of the journey for most people. They get clear on a vision they'd like to manifest. With this, incidents (or challenges) are thrown at them. To progress in their journey, the protagonist must triumph over adversity.

This results in the climax—the part of the story everybody wants to read—the eye-opening, jaw-dropping, inspiring part. Without a challenge, there can be no climax. Without struggle, your story won't progress. If you're going to live out your hero's story, there needs to be an element of resistance. Remember, the goal is to follow a path of least resistance, not a path of no resistance. A path of no resistance doesn't exist. It's an illusion.

When success comes easily to a protagonist, it's not a good story. There's no character development, no substance, and nothing from which to source inspiration and creativity. Think about it like this: your greatest gifts are hidden under a hard, dense web of conditioning. Whenever you face and overcome challenges, you're tearing apart the layers that cloud your essence. Revealing your essence amplifies your creativity.

One of English singer-songwriter Adele's greatest hits, *Someone Like You*, came from a painful, emotional breakup with someone she thought she would marry. The vulnerability portrayed in the song resonated with millions of people and it became one of the most successful tracks of the twenty-first century. Adversity elicits an emotional response you can channel toward your projects. Many people share common struggles. When your art or business reflects these struggles and tells a compelling story, it creates a magnetic effect that attracts people who have had similar experiences. Instead of pain being an anchor that holds you back, leverage it to create something worth sharing.

Heal by Creating

Often, inner struggles can lead us to isolate ourselves. When we feel depressed, for example, the last thing we want to do is expose ourselves to the outside world. However, even these low energy states can serve as an advantage.

Dutch painter Vincent van Gogh struggled with mental illness throughout his life. So much so, that for twelve months between 1889-1890, he stayed in the Saint-Paul-de-Mausole asylum in southern France. The view from his window was filled with rolling hills, cypress trees, and nighttime skies filled with stars. This time of isolation and longing inspired his famous painting, *The Starry Night*. "It often seems to me," van Gogh said, "that the night is even more richly colored than the day, colored in the most intense violets, blues, and greens.... It's clear to me to what depths of loneliness and sorrow, but also what depths of beauty, this night is taking me." The emotional duality he experienced allowed van Gogh to see light in darkness and beauty in pain.

Without dark, there can be no light. Without pain, there can be no beauty. The Universe is circular, and it operates between two poles constantly. Creativity can be born out of success and failure. Regardless of the position you find yourself in, use this to fuel your creativity. Embrace the struggle. It shows you the way.

A big reason my first book was a quick success, despite having had no social media following or public recognition, was because I created it from a place of vulnerability. I spoke from my heart and expressed my thoughts and emotions. Everything in the book resonated with me and helped me overcome my anxiety and insecurity. My healing helped me create, and vice versa. *Creating helped me heal.*

You don't need to have it all figured out. In fact, if you don't, it's easier to be creative. Many artists often stagnate *after* they find success. For them to stay motivated and inspired requires immense effort and a "why" bigger than anything they'll ever be able to achieve during this lifetime. Use your projects as personal development. Use painting, drawing, recording, speaking, building, writing, or editing as a form of emotional expression and processing. By tapping into these states of flow and creativity, you transcend your distress.

To empty your mind, journal. To release stress, draw and color. To let go of tension, dance. Creativity can result in more than just a manifestation—it can be a form of healing. Art can be therapeutic. Through creativity, we manifest physical representations of our inner reality, creating something altogether unique, authentic, and impactful.

Be Inspired by Service

As the saying goes, "God will give his toughest battles to his strongest soldiers." Not only will embracing your struggles make you strong and resilient, it will fuel every project you embark on. A creation from someone who has never struggled will pale compared to the creations of someone who has risen above hardship. Valuable character traits are developed from overcoming obstacles. Instead of running away from difficulties, run toward them—meeting your challenges head on creates a strong sense of self.

The founder of TOMS shoes, entrepreneur and philanthropist Blake Mycoskie, was inspired by the hardships experienced by children in Argentina. While on vacation in 2006, he met a woman delivering shoes to children in an impoverished community. Blake offered to help, and this volunteer experience, called the "Shoes for Tomorrow Project" inspired the creation of TOMS which came from the word "tomorrow." TOMS implemented the "One for One" model, which meant that for every pair of shoes sold, one pair was distributed to someone in need. A little empathy can go a long way and create an idea that changes the world.

For those born into comfortable, privileged circumstances, if you're "struggling to struggle," you might find it difficult to get motivated to reach your goals or derive satisfaction from achieving them. If this is the case for you, look outward. Use your situation and resources to manifest impact. When you develop empathy, it's more likely the struggles of others will inspire you. The natural next step from healing yourself is to heal humanity.

Over the years, readers have reached out to me with questions like, "Ryuu, I don't need more money. I'm fulfilled. I just want to help. How can I help?" This desire to shift from personal success to selflessness marks a significant milestone in the journey toward enlightenment. But to make a truly profound impact, creativity is essential.

Creating large-scale change isn't something you can do alone. You need others' support. For example, if your goal is to plant one million trees by 2030, you can't be the only one planting. There needs to be a movement—a magnetic force that attracts volunteers, workers, and investors. This starts with having a clear, emotional message that touches people on a personal level.

Going back to the TOMS example, Blake Mycoskie had a well-defined, inspiring mission: To use business to improve lives. By creating models and structures that were innovative and sustainable, TOMS distributed over ninety-five million pairs of shoes to children around the world.

Another example is Khan Academy, a free, accessible education platform for students. The idea, from American educator and founder Salman Khan, was sparked when he made simple YouTube videos to teach his cousins math. Since then, it's evolved into a global resource for students in any class or background to improve in subjects like math, science, computing, arts, economics, and more.

Your intention needs to be clear. "I want to help" isn't enough to spark a movement. Typically, clarity around your mission will stem from your own experiences—moments in which you've felt inspired and drawn to provide support to a community in need. When the people you're helping resonate with something you've struggled with and overcome, the emotional energy behind it is powerful. Once you're clear about your mission, the ideas, paths, and epiphanies come (assuming you've applied the concepts from the rest of this book).

Your suffering has a purpose. It's not for nothing. Don't just toss it away. Use it. Leverage it. Take advantage of your story to elevate the dynamics and elements of your creations. Inject them with emotions only you have felt and stories only you can tell. Source your own experiences to create something that only you can create. Irreplaceability isn't just about being unique. It's about having the courage to transform your pain into meaning, and healing yourself and others.

Summary for Chapter 10: Forged by Fire
Law #10: There Is Purpose in Struggle

- **Purpose in Suffering**: Struggles and challenges are part of the journey toward becoming your highest self. Every obstacle you face helps brings you closer to your authentic purpose, with the strength and wisdom earned from overcoming adversity.

- **Your Painful Advantage**: Challenges make the most compelling, impactful stories. Your pain can be leveraged to create something unique and valuable that resonates with others.

- **Healing Through Creation**: Creative pursuits can serve to heal yourself and others. As seen with artists like Vincent van Gogh, your creations reflect your inner healing and growth, turning adversity into beauty.

- **Using Struggles to Connect with Others**: Shared struggles connect people. The emotional vulnerability you channel attracts people who resonate with your story, amplifying the impact of your work.

- **Service as Inspiration**: Shifting focus from self to service can provide inspiration, especially if you're in a place of privilege or feel unmotivated. Helping others who are struggling can facilitate your discovery of a deeper purpose.

- **Transforming Suffering into a Movement**: For those seeking to make a large-scale impact, a clear, emotionally driven mission connects people to your vision, drawing in support and creating a magnetic force around your work.

- **Irreplaceable Creations**: Your unique experiences make you irreplaceable. By channeling your personal pain into your creative work, you produce something that no one else can replicate.

Journaling Prompts

- **Healing Through Creativity:** Reflect on a time when you used creativity (writing, drawing, painting, etc.) to help you process an emotional experience. How did it help you heal or gain clarity? How can you incorporate more of this into your life?

Exercises

- **Turn Pain into Purpose:** Reflect on a painful or challenging experience and identify the lessons it taught you. Now, think of a way to channel that experience into something tangible—whether it's writing, art, a business idea, or a service.

- **Create from Vulnerability:** Spend 20 twenty minutes free-writing about a personal challenge without worrying about grammar or structure. Allow your emotions to guide you. Then, look for key insights or themes you can weave into your creative projects.

- **Empathy in Action:** Choose a cause that resonates with you personally, based on a struggle you've experienced. Brainstorm three ways you could offer support or service to that cause, whether through a creative project, a business idea, or volunteer work.

CHAPTER 11

Trusting the Infinite

◆

LAW #11:

Surrender Is an Act of Creation

When I let go of what I am, I become what I might be.
— **Lao Tzu**

The greatest illusion is the illusion of control—control over our finances, our relationships, even our creative process. But really, we control nothing. We're not orchestrating the Universe; the Universe is orchestrating us.

We have the instruments—our mind and body—but there's a conductor behind the scenes. There's an Intelligence pulling strings, placing signs, and guiding the performance of nature, leading us to more harmony and cohesion. If we're going to be our most creative selves, we must surrender our needs and demands to this higher Intelligence. Every time you try to impose your desires and timing on the Universe, you block magic from happening. The Intelligence is whispering to you constantly, but you need to be aware. Sit back, watch, and listen. The messages can be subtle or sudden. When you let go, you become more receptive to them. When your intentions match the intentions of the Universe, your creative genius shines through. You transcend the physical and become a divine creator.

Natural Mystic

One of my favorite songs of all time is *Natural Mystic* by Bob Marley. If you listen to the lyrics, you'll understand that Bob was aware of a subtle cosmic force that guides us as we assemble the puzzle pieces of our lives. He mentioned the idea of listening carefully to hear the message. Most of us can't hear the messages because we're busy rationalizing our experiences. We ask "Why?" when we should be asking "What?" We look for the root cause of our problems and experiences, using them to manipulate outcomes and make reality predictable. But this futile. We can never truly understand the root cause of anything. Maybe we can blame our difficult circumstances on generational trauma, psychology, or hidden governmental agendas, but beyond that, we're left guessing.

There is a philosophical concept known as *Agrippa's trilemma*. It is the understanding that the question, "Why?" never has an absolute answer. It only leads to one of three places.

- Infinite Regress: Asking why forever.

- Circular Reasoning: Because of A. Why A? Because of B. Why B? Because of A.

- Axiom: An accepted truth, like God, science, or the Big Bang.

Bob in his song also mentions that many will have to suffer and die, and to not ask him why. There can be no concrete explanation for why people suffer or succeed, or why certain things happen or don't happen. We can try to understand this Intelligence with our minds by correlating thoughts with reality, attention with energy, and actions with reactions. However, even with evidence, we can never be 100 percent right. There's an infinite number of nuances to this universal game.

Life is a logical mystery. This means that logically, we understand some causes for some effects, but we can never understand the causes of those causes. Which is why it's a mystery. If you think positive thoughts, you're likely to attract a positive reality. We don't know why. We don't know how. We only know what we know. Therefore, the only thing left to do is to have unshakeable faith that the Universe is taking care of everything. The premise of this book is that we seek to understand—but we will never know.

According to Plato, Socrates once said, "I am the wisest man alive, for I know one thing, and that is that I know nothing." Socrates never gave his followers answers to their questions. He posed questions and allowed the answers to come through him or through the person asking for counsel. It was as though he was operating as an energetic vortex that attracted the right creative insights for the right person at the right time. As referenced by another of his disciples, Xenophon, often, Socrates would receive guidance from a *daimónion,* or a divine voice. Socrates believed his wisdom and creativity was a gift from a deity, and it was his mission to persuade people to prioritize the health of their soul.

A western rationalist could never accept the idea that wisdom and creativity can come from a divine being or voice that's beyond comprehension. For them, Socrates was a rational, analytical, and conceptual genius, not a creative one. However, what made Socrates such a legendary figure was not the knowledge he had, but how he was thinking. He thought creatively, which allowed him to perceive problems, situations, and subjects from a different light than most people were (and still are) accustomed to. We cannot understand the depth of his teachings because we focus on his answers to his students' questions. Answers are only the tip of the iceberg.

Creative thinking isn't so much about coming up with answers as it is about the process through which an answer manifested. What state of consciousness allowed Socrates to access such Intelligence and creativity? It was a state of surrender. A state of allowing the answer to manifest, instead chasing after it. When you can optimize for this surrendered state, the answers that arise carry more weight and relevance.

Creative Timing

Many geniuses and thinkers were ahead of their time, and as a result, they didn't get the recognition they deserved when they were alive. This is because an answer or idea can only be truly impactful when the timing is right, aligning with the flow of the Universe or divine timing. An example of this is Vincent van Gogh. He struggled with poverty his entire life. Legend tells us he sold only one painting during his time on this planet. The people of his era didn't understand the level of genius right in front of them. The innovative style and emotional depth of his work only gained recognition and appreciation after his passing.

With the way we approach our work, it's important to understand the particular philosophy of a culture in a specific timeframe, and to know which way the wind is blowing. However, we must not let others' worldviews affect our creative impulses. We must always dance to the beat of our own drummer, as the saying goes. For example, without creators who think beyond the status quo, where would great innovations come from?

In recent times, there have been many great waves of innovation that have changed the world. In 2017, it was crypto currency and Bitcoin. In 2021, it was the NFT (non-fungible token) market. In 2023, it was ChatGPT and AI. There are waves happening all the time. Those who conceived these world-changing ideas were far ahead of their time—and their ideas took years to take hold. Bitcoin was created in 2009. NFTs began in 2012 – 2013. The term "Artificial Intelligence" was coined in the 1950s. However, it's only now that we're beginning to see the compounded effects of these waves. Those who caught them early generated and experienced great success. Knowing how to catch trends is important and a valuable skill, but knowing which ones to catch is even more critical.

When done unconsciously or driven by ego, catching trends can easily become a distraction from your higher purpose. You may lose yourself in the hype, following delusional crowds or being swept up in manipulative propaganda. Guided by greed and primal urges, this path becomes unsustainable. You might experience fleeting success, but it will never lead to anything truly lasting or meaningful. Anything built on a shaky foundation will eventually come crashing down. In many ways, catching trends without spiritual alignment is akin to gambling.

If an idea pops up in your mind once, it's likely a distraction. If it pops up multiple times over weeks or months, it's likely worth considering. Ideas are like knocks on your door—sometimes just little pranks from kids in the neighborhood, sometimes a delivery of something trivial, and other times a crucial message from a family member that you absolutely need to hear. The persistence of an idea is usually a strong indicator of its validity or value. Following these waves of inspiration and innovation isn't always easy, but it's often straightforward.

There are two ways to align authentically with trends. The first is to realize that not every trend is worth following. When you're genuinely excited about a project and deeply committed, don't let the fear of missing out (FOMO) cloud your judgment and shift your focus. FOMO only breeds stress and dissatisfaction. The excitement and inspiration you feel are signs the Universe is supporting your idea, that the time for your idea has come, and it's seeking expression through you. Commit to this wholeheartedly. Honor it. Give it reverence and appreciation. Don't allow yourself to get distracted by what's happening outside of you. Pay attention to what's happening inside. Let a higher force guide you, rather than trying to follow how it's guiding others.

The second way to catch trends is to surrender to your inner guidance. Trust that your timing is purposeful. It might take longer than it does for others, but that doesn't mean it will be any less fulfilling or impactful. When you follow your intuition wholeheartedly, you might end up pioneering a new path or starting your own wave—or you could be early on catching a wave that's about to rolling in. We can't always predict the timing or outcomes, but one thing is certain: when you align yourself with the desires of the Universe, you transcend the ego and create from a place of real substance. Stay in this space long enough, and eventually, you'll catch a wave so powerful, it will change your life.

You Hold the Truth

Dependency kills creativity. Many of us begin creative pursuits—whether producing a song, starting a business, or writing a book—because of passion or genuine interest. However, often, over time, that enthusiasm fades. Instead of following our hearts, we follow our minds and egos. Our creative pursuit becomes a means to an end: we chase money, status, recognition, or validation. When our creativity depends on an outcome, we disconnect from the essence of true creativity—our divine inspiration. We rely on others for approval or direction, shaping our work to fit what we think the world wants, rather than channeling what flows naturally from within. True creativity emerges when we surrender to the inner voice of our higher self, free from attachment to any outcome.

As Henry Ford once said, "If I had asked people what they wanted, they would have said faster horses." Your audience will always want something new, fresh, helpful, and inspiring, but the only way to give them this is to not listen to them when they tell you what they want. When you listen to outside voices, there's no excitement. No thrill. The only reason to do this is if they want predictability. Otherwise, when it comes to art and creativity, people don't want predictable. They want innovation. They want you to expand their perspective on the subject and their experience of reality.

When you tailor your creative process to fit the world's expectations, you operate from a place of lack, and often, manipulation. Anything produced with this intention will carry an aura of mediocrity and may feel artificial. Listen to your soul—it will give you everything you need to produce at the highest possible quality. Your soul is the only advisor you need to follow.

Ikigai (生きがい) is a Japanese philosophy that helps individuals find their purpose in life. It is the intersection of four distinct elements: what you love, what you're good at, what the world needs, and what you can get paid for. Most people focus only on the last two. Segmentation and separation are not what Ikigai is about. Ikigai is about realizing that your interests and talents *are* what the world needs and allowing them to be the reason you make a living. The outer manifestation of service and success starts by nurturing and expressing the gifts that are within you.

Give yourself credit. Don't become a creative people-pleaser. When everything you create becomes a clutter of recommendations and suggestions, you're not creating—you're following orders. This has no lasting impact on yourself or the world. It's especially common when you see how simple innovation can be.

Often, the simpler the innovation, the more deceiving it is. Because it's simple, we copy, thinking we'll get the same results. Note: there's a difference between copying and modeling. To copy means to reproduce an identical version of something. Modeling is about getting inspiration. Simplicity makes something like a work of art or business difficult to model, but easy to copy.

What most people don't realize is that a unique, irreplaceable energy is embedded in every creation. An example of a simple innovation is the Post-it Note. In 1968, a scientist named Dr. Spencer Silver accidentally created a weak adhesive that wasn't strong enough to meet the standards his company was seeking. It was considered a failure until another scientist, Art Fry, saw potential in the weak adhesive. He used it as a bookmark that would stick to his hymnbook at church but could be removed without damaging the paper. The result was the Post-it Note.

Once invented, it was simple to create and sell, but nobody can copy the Post-it Note. You can innovate on top of it, if possible, but never compete with the original. Universal timing, authenticity, and emotional connection all play a role in innovative ideas.

Does this mean you should never consider outside opinions? Of course not. That would be foolish. There's value in external opinions. They can be simple redirections or collaborations that help you bring your vision to life. But the final say should always come from you. Are you proud of what you've created? As a mentor once told me, "Would you be proud to show it to others and give it to your grandma?" If the answer is no, this is not something you should try to produce. Or it needs work. If you want to feel proud about what you've created, make sure it's coming from within.

The solutions to your creative blocks and goals are not outside of you. They are within you. No one else has ever experienced your unique talents, challenges, or circumstances. Nobody can be you, so nobody can solve your problems. Be your own superhero. Be your own mentor. Be your own coach, teacher, guru, or advisor. Trust yourself to create or not create. This is the path to true creativity.

Full Trust

In the beginning, there's no evidence that what you'll create will make the impact you're expecting. So, it's difficult for the mind to believe in that possibility. When the mind doesn't believe, we're less likely to take action. The way to overcome this hurdle is to do it anyway. It's like planting a seed. For the first few days or weeks, nothing shows. But you trust the Universe. You trust nature. You water and nurture the soil, and the seed sprouts. Creative manifesting works in much the same way. Plant the seed of your work. Nurture it. Experiment with different soils, fertilizers, and watering systems. Once the seed of your idea grows, evaluate the results, then plant the next one. Continue until you become exceptional at planting, and your seeds grow into trees that bear incredible fruit. The easiest way to trust yourself is to become exceptional at your craft. If there's no evidence, *create the evidence*. The work you do becomes the proof you are capable and on the right path.

By creating, you activate a universal feedback loop. Every piece of feedback, every adjustment, and every experiment becomes a calibration device you can use to connect with who you're meant to be and what you're meant to create. You discover a style, voice, and approach that's unique.

Within every one of us is a seed of potential. But we need to water it. We need to energize and attend to it. By trusting ourselves to create based on where we are at today, we connect with the person we desire to be tomorrow. By creating art, we become artists. There's no other pre-requisite. You don't need a degree. You don't need permission. You don't need external validation. The only thing you need is trust that a higher Intelligence wants to flow through you and paint the world with your colors.

Every iteration is an evolution, not a repair or correction. Each project is a stepping stone, not merely a failure or success. When your process becomes the goal, your work reflects something divine. If you distract yourself by seeking validation or hoping for specific outcomes, your neediness will produce misaligned energy which will stifle your creativity. Anything created from this space will radiate neediness and lack self-confidence.

As you create, tap into the deepest parts of yourself, and allow that powerful energy to flow into your work. Expressing yourself fully creates magnetic energy. Remember, however, magnetism has two poles—positive and negative. A work of art that has no magnetism isn't polarizing. Not everyone will resonate with what you are creating—and that's okay. So, to attract raving fans, you must be willing to attract pesty haters. If you try to please everyone, what you create won't bring any new flavor to the world. Art that avoids risk doesn't make the impact it could have made.

Trusting yourself is an act of devotion to the Universe. Honor your gifts. Think back to a time when you were hit with a stroke of genius—a line you wrote, a melody you played, or an idea you channeled. That was your intuition and inner genius speaking. Embrace those moments. Let them guide you. Wear your heart on your sleeve. The more you trust your inner genius and creativity, the more you'll align with the person you're destined to become.

Creative Manifesting is about trust—trusting yourself, the Universe, and what's being expressed through you. It's not about proving anything or one-upping the competition. It's a journey of self-discovery that brings you closer to who you are and connects you to source energy. By amplifying your intuition, you create and manifest a reality that's a direct reflection of the deepest desires of your soul. Every stroke of the brush, every note you play, and every word you write become conversations and collaborations with the infinite. You were born to create at the highest level. Don't let the noise muffle the genius in you.

Summary for Chapter 11: Trusting the Infinite
Law #11: Surrender Is an Act of Creation

- **The Illusion of Control**: True creativity thrives when we let go of control and allow the Universe to orchestrate our experiences. The more we surrender, the more aligned our creative efforts become.

- **Listening to Universal Messages**: The Universe sends subtle signs and messages to guide us constantly, but we need to quiet our minds to hear them. Intuition is the key to unlocking deeper creativity.

- **Move Beyond "Why?"**: Obsessively asking "Why?" leads to either infinite questioning or circular reasoning. By focusing on "What?" and trusting the process, we allow creative insights to flow more freely without the need for full understanding.

- **Creative Timing**: Often, great ideas go unrecognized until the world is ready for them. Trusting in divine timing ensures that your work will make its impact when the conditions align.

- **Aligning with Trends**: Instead of chasing every trend, focus on the trends that resonate with your true passion. This ensures your work stays authentic and aligned with higher purpose, avoiding the trap of following the crowd.

- **Trusting Yourself**: Rely on your inner voice. True creative power emerges when we listen to our intuition and create from within, not from the expectations of others.

- **No Attachment to Outcomes**: Focus on the process of creation rather than fixating on specific outcomes. Detaching from results frees your creative energy and allows the Universe to guide the results naturally.

- **Trust the Process**: Creativity is like planting seeds that take time to grow. Trust that with consistent effort and care, your ideas will blossom when the time is right, even if there's no immediate evidence.

- **Magnetic Energy**: When you create authentically, your work will attract both admiration and criticism. Embrace this polarity, as it shows your creation has substance and uniqueness.

- **Collaboration with the Infinite**: Creating is a partnership with the Universe. By surrendering to this larger force, you channel cosmic wisdom and allow something greater to flow through you.

Journaling Prompts

- **Releasing Control:** Think about a time you tried to control an outcome, and it didn't go as planned. How did that experience shift when you finally let go? How can you apply that lesson to your creative process?

- **Divine Timing:** Reflect on an idea or project that didn't gain the recognition you'd hoped for when you created it. How can you trust in the timing of your work's success, even if it's delayed?

- **Surrendering to Inner Guidance:** When was the last time you followed your intuition in your creative work? How can you listen to and trust your intuition more deeply in your next project?

Exercises

- **Trust the Universe Exercise:** Start your day by setting an intention to surrender. For the next 24 twenty-four hours, pay attention to signs, nudges, or moments of inspiration that arise unexpectedly. Record them in a journal and reflect on how trusting the process led to moments of insight or clarity.

- **Create Without Attachment:** Set a timer for 30 thirty minutes and create something (write, draw, compose) with no end goal in mind. Let yourself flow freely, without worrying about the outcome. Afterward, reflect on how the process felt and what insights or ideas emerged.

A Short Message from the Author

As we wrap up this journey, I just want to take a moment to remind you why this work matters—not only for you but for everyone around you. Each step you've taken here, each insight you've absorbed, is a step towards a more aligned, conscious life. And as you've seen, personal growth doesn't end with us; it ripples outward, lifting the energy of everyone we touch.

Think about how far you've come since the first chapter. You've done the challenging work of expanding your perspective, opening your mind, and perhaps even questioning parts of yourself you once held tightly. That's no small feat—it's the foundation of true progress.

If this book has sparked something within you, please consider leaving a short review. Your review might be the nudge someone else needs to pick up this book and step into a new chapter in their lives, just like my brother's recommendation helped me.

Scan the QR code below to leave a short review.

Thank you for being part of this journey and for your energy in helping create a more awakened world.

With gratitude,

Ryuu

.

Bibliography

Angelou, Maya. Interview by George Plimpton. "Maya Angelou, The Art of Fiction No. 119." *The Paris Review*, 1990.

Anthony, Scott D. *The Little Black Book of Innovation*. Harvard Business Review Press, 2012.

Bergson, Henri. *The Creative Mind*. New York: Dover Publications, 2007.

Berthiaume, André. Quoted in *The New York Times*, December 17, 1971.

Branson, Richard. *Losing My Virginity: How I've Survived, Had Fun, and Made a Fortune Doing Business My Way*. New York: Crown Business, 2011.

Dass, Ram. *Be Here Now*. San Cristobal, NM: Lama Foundation, 1971.

Dylan, Bob. *Chronicles: Volume One*. New York: Simon & Schuster, 2004.

Eno, Brian, and Peter Schmidt. *Oblique Strategies*. San Francisco: Hypergallery, 1975.

Flaubert, Gustave. Quoted in Geoffrey Braithwaite, *Flaubert's Parrot*. London: Jonathan Cape, 1984.

Ford, Henry. Quoted in Anthony, Scott D. *The Little Black Book of Innovation*. Harvard Business Review Press, 2012.

Gibran, Kahlil. *The Prophet*. New York: Alfred A. Knopf, 1923.

Isaacson, Walter. *Leonardo da Vinci*. New York: Simon & Schuster, 2017.

Lao Tzu. *Tao Te Ching*. Translated by Stephen Mitchell. New York: Harper & Row, 1988.

Leonardo da Vinci. *A Treatise of Painting*. Translated by John Francis Rigaud. London: J. Taylor, 1802.

Marley, Bob. *Natural Mystic*. Song lyrics, *Exodus*. Island Records, 1977.

O'Shaughnessy, Arthur. *Poems of Arthur O'Shaughnessy*. Boston: Roberts Brothers, 1873.

Picasso, Pablo. Quoted in Edward Quinn, *Picasso: The Artist's Studio*. Munich: Prestel, 1999.

Proust, Marcel. *In Search of Lost Time*. Translated by C.K. Scott Moncrieff. New York: Modern Library, 1998.

Rowling, J.K. Interview by Oprah Winfrey, "The Oprah Winfrey Show," October 1, 2010.

Tai Xu, Master. Quoted in Thomas Cleary, *The Essential Tao*. New York: HarperOne, 1991.

Van Gogh, Vincent. *The Letters of Vincent van Gogh*. Edited by Mark Roskill. New York: Simon and Schuster, 1997.

Watts, Alan. *The Wisdom of Insecurity: A Message for an Age of Anxiety*. New York: Vintage Books, 1951.

World Health Organization. "Burn-out an 'Occupational Phenomenon': International Classification of Diseases." *World Health Organization*, May 28, 2019. https://www.who.int.

Explore More
of Ryuu Shinohara's
Law of Attraction Series

◇ BOOK 1
The Magic of Manifesting: 15 Advanced Techniques to Attract Your Best Life, Even If You Think It's Impossible Now

◇ BOOK 2
The Magic of Manifesting Money: 15 Advanced Manifestation Techniques to Attract Wealth, Success, and Abundance Without Hard Work

◇ BOOK 3
The Magic of Manifesting Love: 15 Advanced Manifestation Techniques to Stop Chasing, Start Attracting, and Become Magnetic to Your Dream Relationship

◇ BOOK 4
Manifesting with Alignment: 7 Hidden Principles to Master the Energy of Thoughts and Emotions – How to Raise Your Vibration Instantly and Shift to the Frequency of Your Desires

◊ BOOK 5

Accelerated Manifesting: 7 Hidden Secrets to Supercharge Your Reality, Rapidly Shift Your Identity, and Speed Up the Manifestation of Your Desires

◊ BOOK 6

The Myths of Manifesting: 7 Hidden Blocks Stopping Your Manifestation Success and How to Remove Them - Mistakes and Misconceptions Around Reality Creation

◊ BOOK 7

Focused Manifesting: 11 Laws of Manifestation to Master Your Mind and Attention - Stay Consistent and Attract Success in a Universe of Distractions (Includes Exercises)

Scan the QR code below to check out the other books!